AN AMERICAN
JOURNEY BY RAIL

AN AMERICAN JOURNEY BY RAIL

PHOTOGRAPHS BY DUDLEY WITNEY
TEXT BY TIMOTHY JACOBSON

W·W·Norton & Company
New York   London

ISBN 0-393-02621-3

W.W. Norton & Company, Inc.,
500 Fifth Avenue, New York, New York 10110
W.W. Norton & Company, Ltd.,
37 Great Russell Street, London WC1B 3NU

Printed in Italy

1 2 3 4 5 6 7 8 9 0

Page 1: American rail beds and long distances require heavy-duty equipment like this truck, which belongs to a streamlined stainless-steel passenger car.

Pages 2 and 3: A steam train on the Blue Mountain & Reading Railroad in central Pennsylvania evokes a time before the diesel era when trains conveyed the nation's passengers and freight. Now it carries tourists and rail buffs.

Page 4: The last great era of station-building, in the 1930s, produced art deco masterpieces with handcrafted detail, like Newark's refurbished Pennsylvania Station, whose position and function have contributed to the revival of the surrounding area.

Page 5: Freight steam engines were almost always black, but since the diesel era, locomotives have carried the distinctive color schemes and graphics of their owning roads. Here the Santa Fe's latest colors appear on a twelve-wheel high-horsepower locomotive.

Opposite: This gloved brakeman with pocket watch on the *Sunset Limited* at El Paso, Texas, is an image of American railroads that has changed little in a hundred years.

CONTENTS

The monumental proportions of Beaux Art Washington Union Station befit a great national capital. Designed by Daniel H. Burnham in 1908 at a cost of $4 million, and fashioned out of white granite from Vermont, it services all trains north to New York and south and west to Florida and the Mississippi Valley. The memorial is of Christopher Columbus, one of America's earliest travelers.

HE THAT WOULD BRING HOME THE
WEALTH OF THE INDIES MUST CARRY
THE WEALTH OF THE INDIES WITH HIM
SO IT IS IN TRAVELLING. A MAN
MUST CARRY KNOWLEDGE WITH HIM
IF HE WOULD BRING HOME KNOWLEDGE.

Washington Union Station

INTRODUCTION

In the 1920s, a German laborer from Ottawa went to work as a carman on the New York Central Railroad in the border town of Niagara Falls, New York. He inspected the running gear of long freights crossing to and from Canada: journal boxes, air hoses, brakes, flanges, the rest. Hard and honest labor of whose worth in the larger scheme of things he could have little doubt. It earned him, in addition to a modest but decent weekly wage, a pass for travel on the system. Like many men of his time and class, he never went far: trips back to Ottawa or brief sojourns in summer and on holidays to the Adirondacks.

Today people who work for airlines travel on passes to the coast, to the islands, and to big cities. Far is the rule; jets make far possible and, in fact, routine. What people find there is hard to say, and no doubt it varies a good deal. What is not hard to say is that how they get there can hold little charm for them and have slight connection with whatever it is they find when they get there. An airplane is the merest instrument, the purest transportation, which touches nothing between the origin and the destination.

Not so with railroads. As the Niagara Falls carman knew, to ride the New York Central was to become a part of New York — the Empire State just then at its most imperial; to ride the Canadian National was to partake of something distinctly foreign en route to what was after all a foreign capital. It all fit; the scale was right; the possibilities were sufficient, but did not tempt a man to wander too far from his own. He knew what was what.

Some will say this is all a matter of taste, and the judgment of a man who doesn't much like to fly. Perhaps so, but I believe it to be true, and it is what drives the narrative that follows.

It is a narrative about American railroads as they reveal this country to the attentive traveler. This book covers great space — thousands of miles coast to coast, border to border, in one of the world's largest countries, where the fact of great distance has shaped history and explains contemporary behavior. Because it is about railroads, it also embraces many decades of time. Railroads are a nineteenth-century phenomenon, and to travel over them in the late twentieth century is to touch and be touched by many past things. The narrative begins and is anchored, however, in the present: every mile of track traveled by the author and

The Great Northern's vertical lift bridge over the Missouri River in eastern Montana allowed passage of river steamers, while across the deck chugged both Model-As and locomotives.

the photographer in order to compose it can be traveled by the public today. It records a national resource accessible to all, though taken advantage of by too few.

To know a place it is necessary to see a place, and the train affords the fullest vision. We Americans are a rich and powerful people watched by the world, and the keys to our national character and development deserve attention here and abroad. One of the most central of those keys is also one of the simplest: America is a continental nation. It encompasses the great midsection of North America, and is by any measure a very large place. Some 250 million people live here, more than at any time in the past, but for a territory this vast, only a modest number. (One-fifth as many live in Britain, which is one-thirty-eighth the size; half as many live in Japan, which is one-twenty-fifth the size.) Much of the place is empty.

This fact is of great consequence for American railroads and the experience today's traveler has of them. In the nineteenth and early twentieth centuries, when the western two-thirds of America yielded to settlement, the steam railroad was the best means by far for bridging geographical space. So Americans built a vast, far-flung railroad network across spaces where few men then lived. Today other transportation technologies have surpassed the railroad, have stolen the market and our imaginations.

In a commercial republic such as this, one that highly values free choice and free movement, the passenger railroad's moment has long passed. Of the once-giant system, what you see today is only a skeleton, a great cultural resource for sure, but one of little social and no economic utility whatsoever. This means that comparisons (usually unfavorable) with European and Japanese trains, all munificently subsidized and serving densely packed populations, are utterly unfair. It also means that in return for the price of your ticket, you must be willing to take something other than speed or luxury.

That something is the view, and it is a great deal. Long and drawn-out, at fifty miles per hour, it is the view of great space. You experience it in the overnight runs from the Atlantic coast to the Mississippi Valley and the Gulf Coast, in the long land voyages from Chicago to the Pacific. It reminds you that such a vast place could not have been easy to settle; that parts of it still demand much of those who live there; and that as the space filled up (to the limited extent that it did), it filled up with all sorts and conditions of men who left their own peculiar signs behind them. Only the train makes such things clear. Airplanes, by their speed and altitude, diminish all natural proportions. Automobiles, which face you forward toward an unrelenting concrete infrastructure, blind you to them. Only by train is the velocity (the speed and the attitude) right.

What is America like, we asked ourselves, as the railroad reveals it? What do you see out the train window, and why is it worth the considerable time and effort it takes to have a look?

The western railroads refined the publicity shot of a crack train amidst postcard-perfect scenery into a minor art form. Here the Great Northern's *Empire Builder* crosses Two Medicine Creek in Montana in the late 1960s.

"Head-end"—baggage, mail, and express—once represented a major source of revenue in passenger operations. Though reduced from earlier times, the mail is coming back, and checked baggage—loaded by hand from spoke-wheeled wagons—is still a feature of the long-distance passenger train.

Denver Union Station still exudes all the confidence of a time when most people did indeed "travel by train." Its fortune first made when the railroads came in the 1870s and 1880s, Denver lies at the heart of a Rocky Mountain railroad empire.

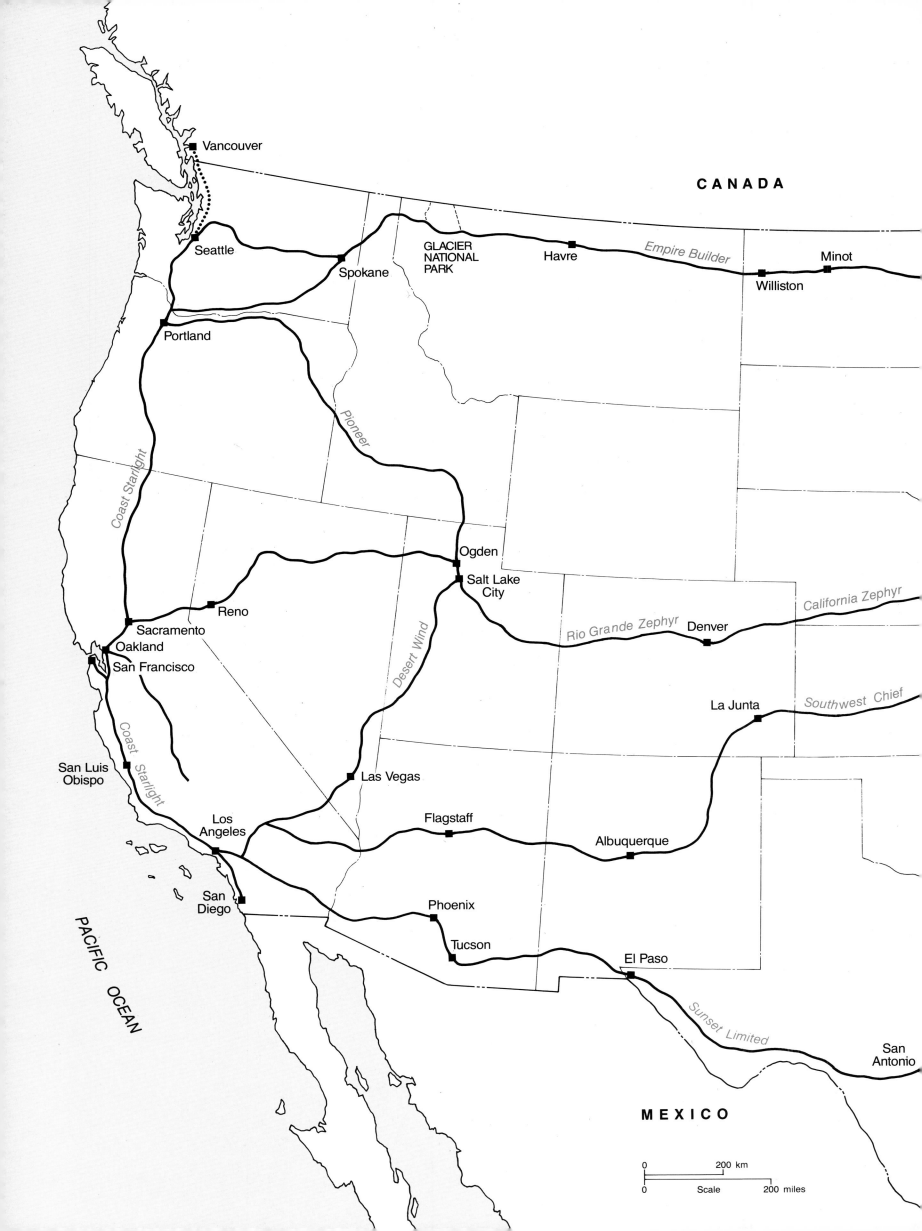

American Journeys by Rail

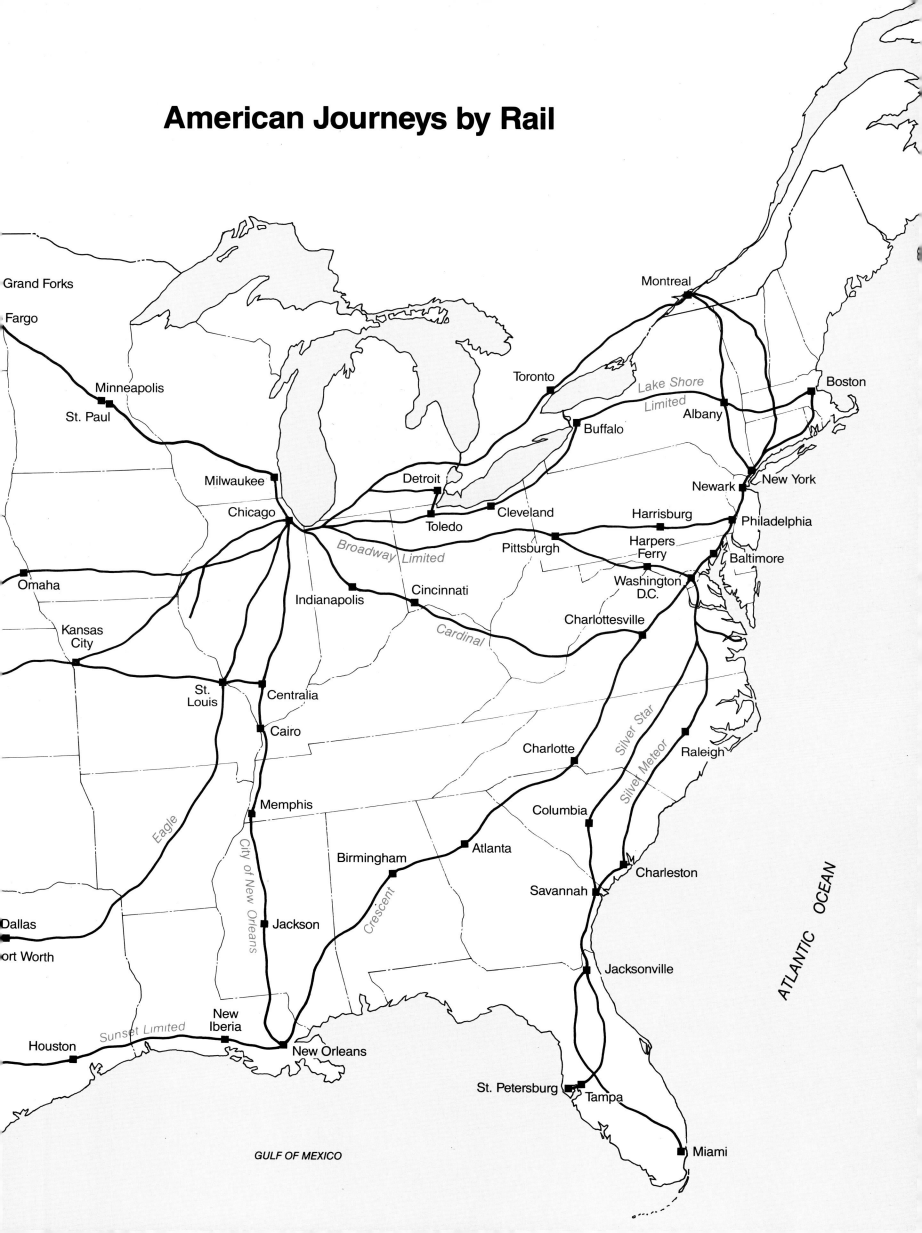

THE EASTERN SEABOARD

Henry Morrison Flagler, partner of John D. Rockefeller at Standard Oil, built the Florida East Coast Railway and with it turned Florida into one of the world's greatest resort destinations.

Long trains of boxcars flanked by telegraph poles were once typical of every railroad in America. Capturing the old image is a Conrail freight along the west bank of the Hudson River near Storm King Mountain north of West Point.

The United States is a continental nation, and for most of its history its energies and attentions have been directed largely inward, focused on achieving economic development and establishing a lasting political union. It lived for years in an age of free security, blessed with weak and friendly neighbors, and isolated behind two vast oceans that it was happy to have policed, at no cost, by the Royal Navy. The story of most of America's railroads is congruent with this historical disposition: the great trunk lines and the transcontinentals ran on the primary east–west axis of national development, and they were integral to its accomplishment.

The coast lines reflect a different orientation, the eastern ones following two of the transportation corridors that diverged from New York and ran, one down the Tidewater, the other above the Fall Line in the Piedmont, southwesterly toward the low natural passage over the southern end of the Appalachians in what is today Georgia and northern Alabama. As once was common with transportation companies, the names of these coastal railroads proclaimed their territorial ambitions and said clearly what they were about. In the East, the Seaboard Air Line and the Atlantic Coast Line competed keenly from Virginia to Florida until their merger in 1967. In the West, the Southern Pacific enjoyed monopoly on that far coast from Oregon to Southern California. Viewed in concert, these three lines define America's edges: they mark where this country begins, and where it ends.

To ride by rail today down the east coast of America is to sense the predominance of what comes at the end of the line over what lies in between. Every day two long streamliners, the *Silver Meteor* and the *Silver Star*, depart New York's Pennsylvania Station bound for both coasts of Florida. They are the descendants of famous limiteds, and while they do a good deal of local work en route, Florida is their real reason for being. As a resort for winter-weary northerners, Florida is the invention of one man, Henry Morrison Flagler, partner of John D. Rockefeller at Standard Oil and a man whose sense of grand design was matched by the fortune he spent in achieving it. Before Flagler, south Florida was a tropical backwater rich with insects and alligators. After Flagler, it was the destination extraordinaire for the North's social and business elite at its zenith: an American Côte d'Azur in every pretentious particular.

Flagler thought, and built, on a proconsular scale. He began fittingly at St. Augustine, founded in 1565 and the oldest continuously inhabited city in North America. There the Ponce de Leon Hotel opened in January 1888. It was a palace that cost $1.25 million in the hard gold coin of that day, and whose Moorish architecture capitalized on the romantic Spanish antecedents of the town. Splendor quickly followed splendor right down the coast, confirming Florida as America's premier winter resort, a title it has held ever since. To Fort Lauderdale, Miami, Biscayne, and especially to Palm Beach with its legendary Royal Poinciana Hotel, came the rich to be with other rich in a charmed, sun-warmed setting that offered a touch of the exotic with all the accustomed luxuries. Flagler's Florida East Coast Railway tied it all together from Jacksonville to Miami in the "Flagler System," which in 1912, a year before his death, reached its apotheosis in a $20-million extension on bridges and causeways out over the keys to Key West. There, on a 1,200-foot-long pier, the Pullmans turned over their passengers to the steamers of the Peninsular & Occidental Line for the ninety-mile sea voyage to Havana.

Of all the trains that through the decades served this resort empire, Flagler's own *Florida Special* set the standard, leaving no doubt that it was a mobile version of the grand hotels its passengers were bound for. For the inaugural run on January 9, 1888, Flagler saw to it that no less a personage than George M. Pullman himself was on board, which was rather like builder George Ismay attending the maiden voyage of the *Titanic*, though this trip had a happier outcome. The *Special*, a Pullman masterpiece, was the first electrically lighted vestibule train in America, its cars named for Flagler's Moorish fantasies: "Alladin," "Alhambra," "Alcazar." The one-dollar dinner featured Salmon à la Chamborg, Roast Leg of South Down Mutton, Fricandeau of Veal, and Saddle of Antelope. Bonfires greeted the *Special* on its night passage to Jacksonville as if to signal the victorious beginning of a new era. So it was: the *Florida Special* lived on for over eighty years as the premier seasonal luxury train to Flagler's empire. In that time it shared distinction with a number of other deluxe trains, which were only a shade less prestigious and which carried, at the peak in the 1920s, a thousand Pullmans every night to and from the Florida resorts.

North of Jacksonville the *Special* belonged to the Atlantic

The Seaboard Air Line enters Sarasota through the swamps of Florida's gulf coast in 1902. One of the great railroad systems serving the resorts, the Seaboard traversed the heart of the South.

Key West, Florida, just ninety miles from Havana, was the most southerly point reached by an American railroad. Henry M. Flagler (center, in the boater), who built the resort town, arrives on the first train into Key West on January 22, 1912.

Coast Line, whose great regional competitor was the Seaboard Air Line. Like the Coast Line, the Seaboard was pieced together from a number of small lines in Virginia and the Carolinas in the 1880s and 1890s and later extended its own tracks south of Jacksonville to both Florida's Atlantic and Gulf coasts. Its answer to Flagler's *Florida Special* was the *Seaboard Florida Limited*, which first ran on January 4, 1903, and counted on its passenger list Andrew Carnegie, the steel king and philanthropist. For the run to Key West over Flagler's causeway, the *Special* and the *Limited* were consolidated at West Palm Beach and renamed, aptly enough, the *Overseas Limited*. But the most fondly remembered and most wonderfully named of the Seaboard's Florida trains dated from the great Florida Boom of the 1920s. This was the *Orange Blossom Special*, christened at Winter Haven in 1925 by young ladies in bathing attire who did the honors with a bottle of orange blossom perfume. It was a train of solid luxuries (club car with barber; ladies' lounge with boudoir), specialized service (porters and dining-car waiters wore armbands with the name of the train embroidered in orange silk), and advanced technology (air conditioning in 1934; diesel power in 1938, the first in the Southeast).

It was the fancy streamliners introduced on the eve of World War II by both the Seaboard and the Coast Line, however, that were destined for the longest careers (the lovely *Orange Blossom*, never streamlined, was withdrawn in 1953), and when you ride to Florida today it is on the direct descendants of these trains. The *Silver Meteor* and the *Silver Star* on the Seaboard and the *East* and *West Coast Champion*s on the Coast Line provided four-times-a-day luxury service year-round to both Florida coasts on parallel routes south of Richmond. Even as rail passenger traffic drastically diminished in the late 1950s and 1960s, these runs, fortified by the steady pull of their tropical destination now on a vastly expanded middle-class constituency, continued to prosper. They still do.

Today Flagler's historic Florida East Coast — "The St. Augustine Route" — no longer carries passenger trains. Riding south on the *Silver Star* from Jacksonville, you travel instead on the old Seaboard mainline right down the center of the state toward Lake Okeechobee and the Everglades. Parts of this landscape resemble the Middle West, and looking out on the open prairies south of Ocala with their grazing herds of cattle and horses may lead to the impression that you are on the wrong train. This middle section of Florida is not what at first made the state a tourist mecca, though in time it came to boast special attractions all its own. Cypress Gardens, near Winter Haven, grew famous for its extravagant water-skiing productions. Sebring played to the car-racing set with its Grand Prix course. A bit to the east on the old Coast Line route now used by the *Silver Meteor*, Kissimmee, Orlando (with its fine old mission-style station, now somehow out of place), and Sanford beckon the Ozzies and Harriets of the 1980s with new and ever-better "worlds" of family fun: Disney World, Sea World, Ringling Brothers and Barnum and Bailey Circus World, and the Kennedy Space Center out on Cape Canaveral. It is not exactly what Flagler had in mind when he built the Royal Poinciana, but it is all product of the same developers' impulse that he understood so well.

Southeast from Okeechobee the railroad runs straight as an arrow for fifty-seven miles to West Palm Beach, which is the beginning of Flagler's Florida, or what you can see of it from a train today. Here the swamps, orange groves, and white egrets give way to urban sprawl. The red-tile station at "West Palm" (as the porter announces it) serves Palm Beach on the ocean just to the east; from Deerfield Beach you reach ritzy Boca Raton; from Fort Lauderdale, Port Everglades, which now sees more ocean liners (all cruise ships, alas, going nowhere) than New York. You can't go to sea by rail anymore, the causeway to Key West having blown down in a hurricane in 1936, so Miami is the end of the line. Ever since the developers first conjured it, the lure of Miami's sunshine, beaches, and palm trees has not changed, whether in the gaudy pleasure palaces of Miami Beach or the sedate twenties elegance of Coral Gables. That elegance, which dates from the great railroad age of the early twentieth century and is so foreign to our own, describes particularly well one other Florida town on the railroad, which like Coral Gables has been engulfed by the booming metropolis around it. Winter Park is for all practical purposes a suburb of Orlando, but it has preserved a fiercely distinct identity with brick streets, small shops, fine gardens. Not unlike the villages along Chicago's North Shore, it shows off to the world an exceedingly pleasant and self-assured prospect, as if to say that this is how life in Florida was meant to be — and in Winter Park still is. The *Silver Meteor* stops briefly here, along a gracefully curved platform in a park with a fountain and a topiary rendering of the station's name. If on a warm summer afternoon you should chance to see there, as I did, a prosperous-looking

In the 1920s a thousand Pullmans a night carried travelers to and from the Florida resorts. From New York all the way to Key West, the lounge car of the *Havana Special* offered wicker, wood paneling, and flappers.

One of the coast lines actually went to sea. The Florida East Coast's overseas extension reached from Miami to Key West over a series of bridges and causeways. Here construction proceeds at Knight's Key in 1908.

couple seated on a park bench with their young children watching the train go through, then you will have had a fine contemporary glimpse of the Florida that Flagler and the railroads built.

Up until its merger with the Coast Line in 1967, the Seaboard had for its logo a circle with a red valentine-like heart in the center of which read, straightforwardly, "Through the Heart of the South." It is an important reminder that while destination governed on these lines, and while the great trains were Northeast-to-Florida affairs, there is also something to them short of Florida. That something is southern. (The Coast Line logo went right on to list all the southern states the road served: Virginia, North and South Carolina, Georgia, Florida, and Alabama.) In better days, even as recently as twenty years ago, numerous secondary maids-of-all-work, like the *Palmland*, the *Cotton States Special*, the *Palmetto*, and the *Everglades*, serviced dozens of small and not so small stations up and down the line. As scheduled today, the *Silver Meteor* and the *Silver Star* pause at relatively few, but still enough to give access to several other Souths.

On the journey south from Richmond over the Seaboard, the *Silver Star* calls at ten stations before reaching Jacksonville early the next morning, a distance of 646 miles. The two most major are both state capitals, Raleigh, North Carolina, and Columbia, South Carolina. Raleigh was named for Elizabeth I's great favorite, Sir Walter Raleigh (whose name also ended up on a pipe tobacco), patron of the unsuccessful attempt to plant the first English colony in America on Roanoke Island in the late 1580s. He fell afoul of court intrigue and the Spanish Armada, and failed. But the failure left behind the legend of the Lost Colony and Virginia Dare, the first white child born in America, and it gave to North Carolina some claim to historical precedence over its haughty neighbor to the north, where a settlement did succeed at Jamestown in 1607. Raleigh the town was established in 1792 specifically as the state capital; it is near the center of this large state and at the heart of its famed tobacco industry.

Train travel sharpens your eye for old things along the way. This is perhaps because the passenger train and the railroad have their roots in another moment of American history. Their presence today serves as a reminder of things we have lost and of other things still with us that we should try hard to save for our children. You can see them in Raleigh in a special place close to the heart of the South's

The Seaboard Air Line's *Orange Blossom Special* beats the clock for a publicity photo at Miami, 1931.

collective cultural memory. That place is the courthouse square, and Raleigh's, which is not far from the station, is an exceptionally fine example. Here it is actually a state capital square, but it renders all the essential elements of the type. The motive is memorial: to venerate the glorious dead, always from the Civil War (or the War Between the States, as southerners still commonly call it), often from other wars as well, in elegiac inscriptions to a lost cause and a fight well fought. Raleigh's square surrounds the antebellum capitol building and presents a giant Confederate column, that ubiquitous set piece of the postbellum South, along with its own special memorials: to the first Confed-

Four *Florida Special*s await departure from downtown Miami in 1927, bound for the Carolinas, Washington, and New York. In the 1920s and 1930s, great trains often ran in several sections.

erate soldier to fall in battle, North Carolinian Hugh Lawson Wyatt, who died at Bethel Church on June 10, 1861; to Worth Bagley, United States Navy, first fallen in Cuba, May 11, 1898; and (the best) "To the North Carolina Women of the Confederacy," which portrays scenes of farewell to a husband bound for battle, of grief at the return of a slain hero, and of resolve to carry on and never forget, in the image of a young boy gripping his fallen father's sword.

Columbia, capital of South Carolina and four stops down the line, was one of the southern cities, like Atlanta, burned to the ground by Sherman's advancing army as the Civil War drew to a close. In later years it joined the New South as eagerly as any other old Confederate bastion, but there are still from time to time echoes of the older sympathies, in what was, after all, the capital of the first state to secede from the Union. For example, a feisty little magazine called *The Southern Partisan* is published here, voicing opinions of a decidedly traditionalist, some would say neo-Confederate, kind. Nowhere in South Carolina is the past far from hand, certainly not in Camden, a little town thirty miles to the north, where in Rectory Park you find a lovely monument not to one but to "Four Camden Schoolboys Who Became Generals in the Confederate States of America." Elsewhere markers commemorate two Revolutionary War battles fought here, both British victories. The railroad station, like the town, is small and evokes yet another southern past, which until the 1960s was the most pervasive one of all. This was once a Jim Crow station, with two sets of ticket windows, waiting rooms, and drinking fountains: one for whites, the other for Negroes. You can still see it (as you can all through the South) if you know how to look. Long an Up Country refuge from Charleston's Lowland fevers and humidity, Camden was known for fine old houses and, as rich Yankees came to play here early in this century, for steeplechases and polo. To this day signs still declare that horses are forbidden on city sidewalks. Camden boldly embraced modern times, too, when E.I. du Pont de Nemours built a large synthetic fibers plant here in the early 1950s, many of whose executives and engineers were familiar faces on the crack Seaboard streamliners that made a fast overnight run up to company headquarters in Wilmington, Delaware.

Charleston, the capital of the Low Country, lies to the east on the old Atlantic Coast Line and is a stop today for both the *Silver Meteor* and the *Palmetto*, a daytime run from New York to Savannah that carries coaches only and makes all the stops. Both Sherman and, for a long time, the modern world passed Charleston by, which does much to account for its lingering charms. The old houses and churches on the Peninsula preserve some of the best of what is left of eighteenth- and early nineteenth-century America, and a stroll around the Battery, where ladies in springtime finery watched the bombardment of Fort Sumter in April 1861 and the beginning of the Civil War, unquestionably does for a southerner what a visit to Lexington and Concord does for a New England Yankee. The walks are paved with seashells, old black men (as if from *Porgy and Bess*, which was set here) still cast for croker and catfish, and out in the harbor long

The Moorish-Spanish fantasies of the Ponce de Leon Hotel capitalized on the historical antecedents of St. Augustine, the oldest continuously inhabited European city in North America. Built by railroad magnate Henry M. Flagler, the "Ponce" and similar grand resorts made Florida the American Côte d'Azur for winter-weary northerners.

obsolescent Forts Sumter and Moultrie silently face the Atlantic. In the hot and dry summer of 1986, salt breezes cooled the water's edge but little else, and natives were heard to say that what Charleston needed most was "for a good hurricane to set itself down off the coast a few miles and just stay there about three days." None did just then, but patience on this coast is always rewarded. The sea is never far: it brings warships to the naval base, banana boats from Costa Rica (just a three-day voyage), and even, still, a few shrimpers.

Part of my run up the Atlantic Coast Line that summer was under special circumstances, aboard the private car of a high official of the line. The car and its presence on an Amtrak train are themselves rich in suggestion for a train traveler in 1986 who remembers train travel from 1956, long before the precipitous decline that led finally to government takeover of the passenger system. To step into the car "Baltimore," a dark green, twelve-wheel, heavy-weight masterpiece, from a modern Amtrak coach (comfortable and well suited as such may be for the market of today) is to be beset by a sense of loss and sadness. It is to return to the 1920s and the greatest days of Pullman Standard, when there were many cars like this, their interior configuration embodying a standard of travel comfort that will not again be repeated. Within its eighty-five-foot length are galley and crew quarters, dining room, sleeping staterooms, observation saloon, and finally the brass-railed open platform. This particular specimen was built by Pullman in 1923 for the uncle of Wallis Warfield Simpson, later the Duchess of Windsor, and it retains today the fittings and the feel of that more ample age: dark mahogany paneling, small yellow carriage lamps, overstuffed furniture. Mechanically updated with self-contained generators, air conditioning, and telephones, it provides a welcome and functional alternative even for the chief executive with a corporate air fleet readily at hand.

It also offers a vantage that is no longer provided in any formal sense on any train in America: the rear view. The Pullman observation lounge car, usually with an open platform, sometimes with an enclosed solarium with rear windows, was once de rigueur on passenger trains of any pretension. Part of the lore of Pullman travel is the memory of sitting in that rearward posture watching, as one watches an open fire or stares at the sea, the track going back. Though the trains grew fewer, the streamlined era kept the faith with superb round-end observation cars with tall windows and rear-facing love seats, the finest of them running on the New York Central's *Twentieth Century Limited*, the Great Northern's *Empire Builder*, and the Southern's *Crescent*, though the Seaboard's own postwar silver fleet featured some very respectable versions, too. I confess not to have stopped in Yemassee, South Carolina, only to have viewed it on a hot summer evening from the rear window of the "Baltimore," which makes its memory secure enough.

The ride in the "Baltimore" also occasioned a remark by my host that resounded far down the years of railroad history and to a conversation with a humbler railroad employee. As manager of a large railroad enterprise, the executive explained that he believed passenger trains gave the railroads that ran them something extra over those that did not. His was obviously a very subjective observation, colored perhaps by his long association with the railroad business. But it confirmed something I had just heard, in a different voice, while talking in the club car of the *Silver Star* between Raleigh and Hamlet, North Carolina, with the longest-running brakeman on the Seaboard (forty-six years on the railroad). He had explained to me what a proud thing it once was to draw a run on the old *Orange Blossom Special*. It was tops, he said, and you knew you were, too, just for being there; it made you happy to be working for the railroad. This man still was happy with his memories and the prospect of just a few more runs before retirement.

The "Baltimore" was coupled to the rear of the *Silver Meteor* in Jacksonville, headquarters of the old Atlantic Coast Line, and it would come off early next morning in Richmond, headquarters of the Seaboard. It is due shortly to find a new home in its first one, Baltimore, which is headquarters of the csx Corporation, now parent of the Seaboard Coast Line and the Chessie System. Built and maintained to last, it no doubt has many useful years ahead riding the rails down the seaboard. Its continuing career bespeaks a certain durableness, which describes the now century-old appeal of these coast line railroads themselves, with their magic tropical destination. Should you see the "Baltimore," it will likely be bringing up the markers of a still very long train bound for Florida "Through the Heart of the South." Tip your hat as it passes.

A Corridor train penetrates a jungle of bridges over the Passaic River, Newark, New Jersey. Position-light signals in the Northeast Corridor reveal the ancestry of this line. The Pennsylvania Railroad is the only electrified long-distance passenger route in America.

Above: Grand Central Terminal, the greatest of the great stations, still stands and still functions— now mostly as a commuters' terminus. Completed in 1913, the station features a unique two-tiered system of track approaches and, over the main hall, a suspended ceiling depicting the constellations of the zodiac. The *Twentieth Century Limited* is long gone, but the station's information booth and the oyster bar are still rendezvous for the thousands of New Yorkers who pass through every day.

Right: A turbo train en route from New York City to Albany skirts granite and concrete cliffs along Harlem River at Spuyten Duyvil.

Webs of copper catenary hang
above a modern electric locomotive.
Underground rails provide key
access to Manhattan for New York
City's millions. Electrified early in
the century, the approaches to Pennsylvania Station are the busiest rail
passenger arteries in America.

From the Lackawanna terminal in Hoboken, New Jersey, across the Hudson River from Manhattan, the fabled *Phoebe Snow* once followed the "Route of Anthracite" to Binghampton and Buffalo. Today the station's copper-clad facade, cobbled forecourt, clock, and waiting room see only commuters—and they don't like to wait.

Larger stations have always sold
things other than tickets—papers,
shoeshines, haircuts, and, here in
Hoboken, bargain-priced nectarines.

Maintenance-of-the-way equipment:
this additional station scenery at
Hoboken, New Jersey, is much
beloved by railroad modelers.

Above: A Metroliner pauses in Newark, New Jersey. In the Northeast Corridor between New York City and Washington, D.C., where speed is of the essence, Amtrak competes successfully with other forms of passenger transport. Today's Amfleet equipment resembles an airline's fuselage without the wings.

Right: Sunshine filtering through the skylights accentuates the strong riveted forms of posts and girders at Newark's Pennsylvania Station.

"In 1903, the Wright brothers
invented the airplane.

Above: When railroads were king in the late nineteenth century, their presidents acted the part. The Pullman Company built this private car for Austin Corbin, president of the Long Island Railway from 1889 to 1890. The car is now preserved at the Adirondack Museum in Blue Mountain Lake, New York.

Right: Railroads commissioned some of the most innovative architecture of the nineteenth century, some of it happily preserved. This fine roof graces the Baltimore & Ohio roundhouse in Baltimore, now a railroad museum. The former Mount Clare Station (part of the complex) was the first railroad station in America.

Above: The private railroad car, once widely used by the wealthy for business and pleasure, has lately enjoyed a revival; several hundred operate, with a variety of staff and amenities. The view from a rear open platform is the best.

Right: Summer service to Cape Cod over the old New Haven Line recalls the era of train travel to other seasonal resort areas all over America. This 544-foot span of the lift bridge over the Cape Cod Canal at Buzzard's Bay is the second-longest in the country.

American mechanical engineering at its most exuberant: the Pennsylvania Railroad's GG1 electric locomotive, styled by Raymond Loewy, was used between New York City, Washington, D.C., and Harrisburg, Pennsylvania, from the mid-1930s until the 1970s.

Yankee ingenuity brought rails to the top of Mt. Washington in New Hampshire (6,288 feet) in 1866. The world's first mountain cog railroad with grades up to 37 percent, it continues to operate with 100 percent steam locomotion.

The sensation of speed is more
apparent on a fast train than on any
other form of mass transportation,
as seen here, from a rear car over
welded rail and concrete ties near
Providence, Rhode Island.

The *Silver Meteor,* seen here at Delray Beach, and the *Silver Star* link the Northeast to Florida's subtropics, with fast overnight schedules.

Train travel can take you down
the middle of the street in a small
southern town; here, Ashland,
Virginia, is viewed from the
Silver Star.

Miami's ultramodern elevated
system will soon connect its long-
distance passenger station with
a revitalized downtown.

Above: A now little-used door in the Spanish-style station at West Palm Beach.

Right top: Traveling south on the *Silver Star* one awakens in central Florida to the world of citrus groves.

Right bottom: The end of the line: Miami, as far south as you can go by train in America. The *Silver Star* is readied for its return to the north from Amtrak's new station.

THE TRUNK LINES

No other railroad station in America (and few in the world) has about it the aura that enfolds Grand Central Terminal in New York City, and none has more often been the subject of etchings, paintings, and photographs.

The Lackawanna system linked the Hudson River with Pennsylvania, New York State, and Ohio. On it is the world's largest reinforced concrete viaduct: the bridge over Tukhammock Creek at Nicholson, Pennsylvania, which was 2,375 feet long and 240 feet high. This sister bridge is located farther up the valley.

Ah, New York! Wall Street, Broadway, Fifth Avenue, Central Park, the Yankees, the Met, Carnegie Hall. No doubt about it, New York stands out: one of the greatest cities in the world and the greatest in America. For that distinction it owes much to the accidents of geography. Its great harbor is the finest on the Atlantic shore, and for the centuries when the commerce of the world was seaborne, New York beckoned tall ships and liners and established its preeminence. It had ready access to the larger world, in whose image it made and remade itself.

It was a habit that continued into the airborne age; while its access is no longer exclusive (as it was when the *Queen Mary* docked in Manhattan and no place else), New York still is the place to and from which most of the rest of the world comes and goes. It also has always had water access to America, up the Hudson, the Mohawk, the Erie Canal, the Great Lakes, and into the continental interior. But even though much of its early wealth came from brokering inland produce, New York always looked steadfastly eastward to find itself.

Perhaps for this reason, New York never seemed a great railroad town as Chicago did. True, it was home to two of the finest train stations ever built, but New York was an endpoint (or a beginning) not a junction, which was where railroads really made their mark. Skyscrapers, great ships, bright lights: these, not trains (unless they were subways), symbolize Manhattan. It was Chicago where the nation changed trains. Between the two, the glamour of New York and the solidity of Chicago, you had all that was best in American cities. It was fitting therefore that they once were joined by what the New York Central Railroad touted as "The Most Famous Train in the World," and the train that the Pennsylvania Railroad, its competitor, maintained longer than any other in deluxe all-Pullman status.

Nine-hundred-plus miles of railroad connect New York and Chicago, roughly as many as from London to Warsaw, or from Paris, through Switzerland, down to the boot of Italy. To travel by train between New York and Chicago even today captures something of the cities' old "big time" status. The trains — the *Lakeshore Limited* and the *Broadway Limited* — are long and busy, and though less prompt than they once were, they do the distance on overnight schedules

meant for the convenience of New Yorkers and Chicagoans, and not for people in between. There is in fact no "bigger time" than the place where the *Lakeshore* begins: Grand Central Terminal, opened in 1913 at 42nd and Park Avenue as a functioning monument in the French Renaissance style to the great age of trains. Object of numerous preservationist vs. developer disputes, it still serves its original purpose, though few long-distance trains call there anymore.

The *Lakeshore* is the longest of the trains using Grand Central. Emerging at 96th Street from the Park Avenue tunnel, it follows for the next 140 miles the east bank of the Hudson River to Albany, and provides one of the loveliest train rides anywhere in the world, passing (in season) West Point and Storm King Mountain at sunset. Remains of Dutch New York linger in the names: Spuyten Duyvil, Yonkers, Stuyvesant, Kinderhook. At Hyde Park, the Dutch-descended Roosevelts made their family seat. Nearby, the Vanderbilts, railroad tycoons of the first order, made theirs. Into the 1950s, one of the New York Central's best New York–Chicago trains was called the *Commodore Vanderbilt* after Cornelius Vanderbilt, who made his first fortune in the steamboat business before the Civil War. After the war, the Commodore, as he became known, went on to larger things, chiefly the creation of the New York Central Railroad out of various competitors, piling up a mammoth fortune as he did so.

The Illinois Central (IC) arrived in Chicago in the 1850s and was built along much of the lakefront. Central Station, just south of the Loop, was the northern terminus for the IC's trains from the South, including the *Panama Limited*. Central Station is seen here in 1894, the year after the great World's Columbia Exposition. It was demolished in the 1970s.

Depicted here in a bygone Manhattan cityscape free of skyscrapers, Grand Central Terminal to this day gracefully weathers urban change and stands majestically amid the less imperial architecture of a modern age.

The New York Central, whose tracks up to Albany and west to Buffalo these once were, was for nearly a century one of the giants of American railroading and of American business generally. It blanketed New York State, reached east into New England, west along the Great Lakes to Chicago, north into Michigan and Canada, south and west to Cincinnati, Louisville, and St. Louis. The slogan emblazoned on its timetables and calendars capitalized on this geography, particularly the route to Chicago: "The New York Central System: the Water Level Route — You Can Sleep." It happened to be true. The Central did follow the water: the Hudson, the Mohawk, Lake Erie, straight, smooth, and fast, to the Midwest. It was also a nice slap at the competition, the mighty Pennsylvania, implying that the Pennsy's steep grades and curves through the Allegheny Mountains posed some obstacle to contented repose. It iş a point long lost, and Amtrak, which today operates trains on both routes, makes no distinction.

The *Lakeshore* reaches Buffalo, New York, in the wee hours, thence hugs the south shore of Lake Erie through Conneaut, Ashtabula, Cleveland, Elyria, Sandusky, and Toledo. The last lap, across northern Indiana, comes in daylight. It passes Elkhart (a division point graced by an old New York Central steam locomotive), South Bend (home of the University of Notre Dame), Indiana Harbor and Gary (with their mills), Whiting (with its refineries), South Chicago, and then Chicago itself. The journey, from the heart (or the bowels) of Manhattan to the great metropole of the Midwest, covers 960 miles and consumes eighteen and a half hours, a good two hours more than when things on the New York Central were still at their peak in the early 1950s, and about seventeen hours more than the jets that today carry all the expense-account trade between New York and Chicago.

Time is money. But so it has always been, and there was a time when this fact also mattered to the railroads who ran the passenger trains. So, just seven miles south of Chicago's Union Station, Englewood reminds us. The neighborhood has changed, as they say, and Englewood today is a ruin. But it once served as an important stop for Chicago's South Side. Fifteen minutes after leaving downtown the great limiteds paused here to entrain passengers for the East. It also served as something of a starting gate for an unsanctioned but frequent race, along several miles of parallel right-of-way, between the two finest and most famous trains ever to connect New York and Chicago: the New York Central's *Twentieth Century Limited* ("The Most Famous Train in the World"), and the Pennsylvania's *Broadway Limited*. Racing, strictly against the rules, was irresistible, and there are fine old photographs of the two trains, hell-bent for New York charging out of Englewood — racing.

The *Lakeshore* is today's shadow of the famed *Twentieth Century*, which was introduced in 1902 as the train "a century ahead of its time." It ran continuously for sixty-five years (it died the same year, 1967, that Cunard's Queens left the Atlantic), and for social cachet and sheer luxuriousness of accommodation there was never anything quite like it. "A fine gentlemen's club on rails," it carried all the great and famous and welcomed them with a 260-foot red carpet that was rolled out for each and every departure. It had the right of way over everything on the system. Every week, Henry Luce entrusted to its mail car the pictures and editorial layouts for *Life* magazine, which was edited in New York but printed in Chicago. It inspired *The Twentieth Century*, a Broadway hit in 1932 by Ben Hecht and Charles MacArthur of *Front Page* fame, which was revived in musical form in the late 1970s to rave reviews.

Theatrical associations have also become attached (mistakenly) to the other great train between America's two greatest cities. The Pennsylvania's *Broadway Limited*, like the *Twentieth Century*, began life early in the century when all things connected with railroading were bright and

Cornelius Vanderbilt originally made his fortune in steamboats in the mid-nineteenth century, but later founded the New York Central system and became one of the greatest railroad tycoons of all time. As much as any, his name was synonymous with the wealth and power of the railroad age.

expectant. The Pennsy proudly styled itself "The Standard Railroad of the World," and since it was the biggest railroad company in America (and for a time the biggest American corporation of any description), the boast made sense. The Central followed the water west to Chicago; the Pennsy attacked geography more directly (and its route ended up fifty miles shorter). Westward from Philadelphia and Harrisburg, the mainline flung itself across the spine of the Allegheny Mountains, around the legendary Horseshoe Curve, to Pittsburgh. Everything about it was heavy-duty: the motive power needed for the grades, the rolling stock, the distinctive position-light signaling system, and the track itself. A four-track mainline (six between New York and Philadelphia) carried dozens of passenger trains and heavy freights through the coal and steel country of America's Ruhr, and it is from this generously proportioned right-of-way (and not New York's theater district) that the *Broadway* gets its name.

The *Broadway* was the Pennsy's finest — "Leader of the Fleet," as the brochure given to every passenger even in the 1960s put it. And in either its old Pullman Standard dress of the 1920s and 1930s, or the tuscan red livery of the streamlined era that began with the Raymond Loewy–designed *Broadway* of 1938, it was a fitting, no-nonsense symbol for a truly great railroad. If in the great contest of prestige and glamour it never was quite a match for the *Twentieth Century*, the *Broadway* does get the credit for lasting longer and for sustaining, long after it made any economic sense, deluxe and exclusive all-Pullman status. It carried a wonderful array of sleeping accommodations, including, in addition to the usual roomettes and bedrooms, duplex single rooms (compact up-and-down affairs for one, with a crosswise bed and private facilities), and two master rooms, which were the pinnacle of Pullman private-room luxury, with two lower berths, wood paneling, and private showers. Pullmans trailed the mail car; a twin-unit diner and midtrain lounge followed, then more Pullmans and the observation car, whose lighted tail sign depicted the Pennsy's namesake "broad way." The schedule matched the accommodation: a 6:00 P.M. departure from Pennsylvania Station in New York and a prompt 9:00 A.M. arrival in Union Station in Chicago. Cocktails, a fine dinner, a restful night, breakfast with the paper — and the traveler arrived ready for a day of business in the Loop.

Today it is, of course, a bit different. The name happily endures; the route is unchanged; the schedule is slower.

Midafternoon departures truncate the business day, but then businessmen don't travel by sleeper anymore anyway. But for those who choose to, the *Broadway* is still a good way to go. (It is especially so from Philadelphia, which has a better, 4:20 P.M. departure, or from Paoli, half an hour west on Philadelphia's mainline.) The consist (the train's cars) is full-service by Amtrak standards and serviceable enough, and like many eastern trains outside the New York–Washington corridor, it is made up partly of streamlined cars built in the 1940s and 1950s. That none was built for the Pennsy's old *Broadway* (but for the Union Pacific, as it turns out) seems a fine point, for they still evoke something of the feel of the train's haughty predecessor. Out over the old eastern mountains, first crested by white men in the eighteenth century, it carries you: Lancaster (center of rich farms), Harrisburg (where the overhead electrical wires end), the viaduct over the Susquehanna (the longest stone arch bridge in the world), Altoona (site of the Pennsy's once great car and locomotive shops), the Horseshoe Curve (completed in 1854 by slicing off the side of a mountain using nothing but human and animal power), Johnstown (of flood fame), Pittsburgh (where they still make steel). Early morning brings a race across the flatness of northern Indiana, and, on the last lap into Chicago (just as on the *Lakeshore*), the mills of Gary.

These aging steelworks mark the effective western limits of the nation's industrial expansion. Along this river, lakeshore, transmontane axis, Americans in the nineteenth century built the greatest workshop of the world, which, unlike the British version, was also the most lasting one. New York and Pennsylvania were for years our richest and most populous states, with Ohio, Michigan, and Illinois not far behind. Not so long ago, it could fairly be said that if it wasn't made in Chicago, or New York, or someplace in between (Gary, Detroit, Syracuse, Rochester, Toledo, Fort Wayne), well, then, it mustn't have been invented yet. At one end of the axis, New York and Philadelphia were industrial, mercantile, polyglot, and big; so, in every respect but age, was Chicago at the other end. Somewhere between them, the East becomes the Midwest with Chicago at its center.

Back in New York an old lady was overheard to ask her brother, an aged priest from Buffalo, if the statues overlooking Park Avenue atop Grand Central Station were the likenesses of saints. (They aren't.) In Chicago, nuns and small boys stroll beneath Union Station's Corinthian

The New York Central traveled up the Hudson and Mohawk valleys and along the Great Lakes to Chicago ("The Water Level Route—You Can Sleep"). Its 1938 timetables advertised two of the wonders along its route, one man-made—Grand Central Terminal—and one natural —Niagara Falls.

NEW YORK CENTRAL SYSTEM

TIME TABLES

New York Central
Michigan Central
Big Four Route
Pittsburgh & Lake Erie
Boston & Albany

Niagara from Falls View

The Water Level Route -- *You Can Sleep*

EFFECTIVE JUNE 15, 1938, FORM 101

NEW YORK CENTRAL SYSTEM

TIME TABLES

New York Central
Michigan Central
Big Four Route
Pittsburgh & Lake Erie
Boston & Albany

Grand Central Terminal, New York City

The Water Level Route -- *You Can Sleep*

EFFECTIVE JUNE 15, 1938, FORM 101

arcade, and it could be a cathedral. (It isn't.) But these places and the railroads that join them are this: symbols of cultural confidence and power born of another age and another faith, which (also like the trains that join them) make the transition to modern times and sensibilities rather poorly. Grand Central is a commuter terminal filled with off-track betting windows (although the Oyster Bar restaurant still prospers there). Union Station was half-demolished twenty years ago and could use a good wash (it has no restaurant at all). Few foreigners see these things anymore, traveling as they do by plane. Few Americans see or seem to remember them either.

If you are among the relative few who do choose to travel this way, and when you next alight in Chicago from the *Lakeshore* or the *Broadway*, look around at a city the likes of which they don't build anymore. Immortalized by player-with-railroads Carl Sandburg and a lot of other subsequent proletarian bards, Chicago trades, makes, and builds things: a straightforward place where pretense doesn't get you far. Railroads were once a big part of it.

There is something special about beginning a train trip in Chicago, even after the classic run from New York. While everything about New York demands an international context, Chicago is mere American and always will be, despite promoters' efforts to attach to its durable old imagery the dubious distinction of "world class." No: from its beginnings as a prairie encampment, through its growth as a railroad and stockyard boomtown and a steelmill and skyscraper metropolis, the great sprawling city by the lake is American to the core.

The feeling extends to the great railroads that spring from it, most of all to the Illinois Central. To journey the length of its mainline, which begins on Chicago's lakefront, is to traverse the heart of the American nation in geographical place and historical time, as no other journey comes close to doing. Shooting straight down the Illinois prairies and coal fields and then paralleling the Mississippi River to New Orleans, the IC (now merged with the Gulf, Mobile & Ohio, it is the ICG) connects two far ends of American culture. Midwestern Yankee Chicago, Latin francophile New Orleans, and the vast rural spaces in between and so unlike either are proof at a glance of the possibilities latent in the idea of a pluralistic federal republic, itself an American invention. At the end of your journey next day, you find yourself nearly a thousand miles from where you started, in the tropics — and still in America.

When steam was king, the New York Central's 4-6-4 "Hudson" locomotives were the pride of the Water Level Route, named for the great river whose east bank they traveled between New York and Albany.

Stephen A. Douglas, an Illinois senator in the 1850s, is famous for his debates with Abraham Lincoln over slavery in the western territories. He also sponsored generous federal grants of public land to subsidize railroad building, a policy that was key to railroad expansion until the end of the nineteenth century. The Illinois Central received the first such grants, in 1850.

Emblazoned on the sides of old boxcars, the famous IC slogan aptly describes this railroad: "The Mainline of Mid-America." From the Great Lakes to the Gulf of Mexico, the Illinois Central bisects the country. It was born in the tumultuous 1850s and was actually two lines, one reaching south from Chicago to Centralia, another coming down from Dunleith on the Mississippi. The fifties was a decade marked by the twin fervors of western expansionism and antislavery agitation, the combination of which in time drove the nation to civil war. Real magic attached to railroads then, especially in the West where they were viewed as catalysts to settlement of those vast spaces. A direct result of that spirit, the IC became the first railroad to benefit from a special form of congressional largesse that had helped finance many earlier internal improvements. In September 1850, the year of the Great Compromise that saved the Union for another ten years, President Millard Fillmore signed into law the bill granting the IC (and the Mobile & Ohio Railroad in Alabama and Mississippi) six alternate sections of land per mile of track. It was an important precedent, vital to the rapid construction of the western rail system in the late 1860s, 1870s, and 1880s, when settlement and hence revenue traffic were still sparse. All told, more than 130 million acres from the public domain passed to the railroads, most of them prairie roads like the IC and nine-tenths of them west of the Mississippi. Senator Stephen A. Douglas was the dogged sponsor of the IC land grant. Another Illinois lawyer of note with an IC connection, Abraham Lincoln, once argued and won a key tax case for the railroad — and later sued them for his fee.

With some seven hundred miles of track when it was finished in 1856, the IC was perhaps the longest railroad in the world, and in time its reach extended far beyond its namesake prairie state to Kentucky, Tennessee, Alabama, Mississippi, and Louisiana. Indeed, if the IC over the years could be said to have had a special character, that character was surely southern. It was places like Memphis, Jackson, Vicksburg, and New Orleans that gave the IC its working image and not a little of its traffic. So the management in offices at Michigan Avenue at 11th Street in Chicago acknowledged, with a fleet of passenger trains called *Creole, Louisiane, Seminole, Chickasaw, City of New Orleans, Panama Limited*.

The character endures. The overnight (and the only) run to New Orleans today is on Amtrak's *City of New Orleans*, a name that originally belonged to a deluxe all-coach streamliner that covered this ground on a fast daytime schedule. The great night train was the all-Pullman *Panama Limited*, whose club car stocked at one count forty-two brands of bourbon and whose diner purveyed fare redolent of dinner at Antoine's. Its exotic name dated to 1911 and the IC's effort to cash in on the prestige of the recently completed Panama Canal, one of the wonders of that age and a very American one at that. Today the wonder and indeed the canal are gone (or soon will be) from American hands, so it is probably just as well that this train is now known by the name of the city 924 miles down the track, a city that still does have some wonder about it. It is a distinguished name, one that inspired a dandy Arlo Guthrie ballad in the 1970s, and one that is, of course, indubitably southern.

For a journey over the IC, this one begins out of place, in Chicago's Union Station, which since the coming of Amtrak truly is that: one station for all long-distance trains serving the city. One of the first of Chicago's railroads, the IC long ago managed to preempt much of the lakefront from downtown all the way to 49th Street, and from the 1890s until the early 1970s all its trains used picturesque old Central Station on Michigan Avenue. (The station is now gone, but IC commuters still use a lakefront facility just to the north.) Now, to reach the mainline from Union Station requires a backing operation and transit of what is known as the St. Charles Airline, a short stretch of track that connects with the IC at 16th Street. It also affords, if you have a roomette on the left side of the train, one of the best views ever of the Chicago Loop. The journey south comes quickly; the IC for the next 200 miles is a prairie speedway of a railroad. But still in Chicago it passes two especially historic scenes: John D. Rockefeller's University of Chicago, built on the site of the World's Columbian Exposition of 1893, and three miles farther on the backside of Pullman, once the factory town where the man who gave his name to this most marvelous of conveyances built thousands of the things.

Then comes the prairie at eighty miles an hour, which at an altitude of eight feet is immeasurably faster than five hundred miles an hour is at thirty thousand feet. Train travel keeps you in touch, both with what you see out the window and with those you have ample time to meet. On this particular evening there was a young couple in the diner returning to Springhill, Louisiana, from a vacation in Nebraska. New to train travel, they were happy to learn something more about the origins of Amtrak, whose name was on the ticket, about the IC, whose tracks these were,

The Illinois Central's all-Pullman *Panama Limited* poses in front of Chicago's Michigan Avenue and the Conrad Hilton which, in the early postwar years, was still the largest hotel in the world.

and about the forty-year-old dining car with etched glass panels they were riding in. In return (they were commercial photographers) they made plain the real meaning of the collapse of oil prices in an energy state like Louisiana. Most customers, they explained, had cut back from the ten-dollar to the seven-dollar school package — and the three dollars made a difference. But the train, they said, was much more comfortable than the bus and cheaper than the plane. So they defined the modern market for the passenger train in America.

The market for the *City of New Orleans* today appears to be largely black, which is in keeping with the key role played by the IC route in one of the greatest migrations of Americans from one part of their country to another. For sixty years, from before World War I right up through the 1960s (that is, for as long as Chicago prospered and offered jobs), the IC was one of the main arteries carrying poor but aspiring black southerners on "The Flight Out of Egypt" (as the Chicago *Defender* called this mass movement) north to Chicago, to more money, and to better lives. For many, the first glimpse of the promised land came as they got off the train at the IC's Woodlawn Station at 63rd Street, port of entry to Chicago's South Side, which is still sometimes referred to, accurately enough, as North Mississippi. Today the migration has all but stopped, but there remains a high volume of to-ing and fro-ing between the South Side and places like Memphis, Tennessee, and Canton, Mississippi, as the passenger load in the coaches of the *City of New Orleans* readily attests.

The geographic as well as the sociological South also begins while you are still in Illinois. The state's hilly bottom third was settled before the Civil War by pioneers from Kentucky and Tennessee who brought with them (and whose descendants have sustained) the accents and attitudes that make this Dixie in everything but official jurisdiction. At Effingham, which is about the dividing line, young black boys shoot baskets on an unlit school court at trackside; at Centralia (railroad-named: at the center), where the train waits an hour for a connecting section from Kansas City and St. Louis, great old-fashioned fans in the station waiting room do nothing to ease the 90°F. heat of the night. Crew talk is of heat, bugs, and families back home. The historical South begins a bit farther on, where Mark Twain said it did: where the Ohio empties into the Mississippi at Cairo (pronounced Kay-ro), Illinois. The *City of New Orleans* passes through in the wee hours, and if you doze and miss it you find yourself next morning, like Nigger Jim in *Huckleberry Finn*, down the river and past the free states for good.

One of the revived amenities of traveling by Pullman is the morning newspaper, which the porter brings to your door, in this instance the Memphis *Commercial Appeal*, a venerable sheet dating back to 1840, the heyday of the Cotton Kingdom. King Cotton has long since been dethroned here, but to the attentive watcher from a train window coming into Memphis, sad remnants still proclaim him: the backs of disused cotton warehouses on one of whose walls "R.J. Barton, Cotton Factor" advertises himself to trains and vanished steamboats along the river. Today in Tennessee other images are as compelling. "Farm Grown, sir, or original?" asks a front-page headline of this particular morning's *Commercial Appeal*: "The boss fish of the Tennessee River has got to be an eye-popper. For when it comes to catfish, this is the mainstream."

The real stream from Memphis south, however, is the Mississippi, visible from the west side of the train. Having discharged a hefty contingent of blacks (seeking southern "connections" or returning from Chicago ones), the *City of New Orleans* seeks its Delta. This is the fecund land of Faulkner's Yoknapatawpha County and Will Percy's *Lanterns on the Levee* — and the land that so many southerners have forsaken for places like Chicago, aboard the IC. Through Batesville, Grenada, and Durant, Mississippi, the landscape of the Delta takes over: fields, forests, swamps, sluggish streams with Indian names, crop-dusting planes, the ruins of sharecropper shacks that remind you of a past order of things, small children on screened-porch swings who assure you of an unchanging one. It was at Vaughn, Mississippi, fourteen miles north of Canton, that the most famous of locomotive engineers, Casey Jones, met immortality by crashing into a stalled freight train. Forty miles west of the mainline from Jackson lies Vicksburg, site of the great Civil War siege and, along with Natchez, the quintessential river town. Once upon a time Vicksburg was joined to Memphis and New Orleans by the Yazoo & Mississippi Valley Railroad (part of the IC system), and the best-named of all Illinois Central trains: *The Planter*.

At McComb, the last stop in Mississippi, vines grow over the lampposts, and crepe myrtle, Spanish moss, and strange-sounding little towns — Osyka, Tangipahoa, Amite, Tickfaw, LaBranch — soon announce that this is Louisiana. At Manchac the train skirts on causeways between lakes Maurepas and Pontchartrain. The last lap of the journey

The conductor and engineer of an Illinois Central passenger train exchange schedules. In 1948, diesel locomotives were the latest railroad wonder, and trains still carried more people by far than planes.

parallels the old Airline Highway (it went to the airport long before the interstate did), where visual riches of a distinctly Louisiana sort can be enjoyed in profusion: London Lodge Motel, Bayou Plaza, a jumbo billboard from which "Orleans Parish Sheriff Charles Foti invites you to Santa's Workshop." Welcome to New Orleans.

To the wider world New Orleans is known chiefly for fine food and political corruption rivaling even Chicago's. During my stay the *Times-Picayune* carried a story uniting these two historic themes. The outgoing Orleans Parish grand jury, it seems, had entertained on a public voucher the incoming grand jury to a rather lavish, even by New Orleans standards, luncheon at Broussard's in the French Quarter. The bill for twenty-four jurors came to just over $4,400, $1,920 of it for champagne, $64.50 for cigars. The paper groused but, New Orleans–style, the people paid. The place also has other charms, including some little-known railroad lore. I am indebted to my hosts, old friends whose family have lived there since before the Civil War, to learn that the first railroad laid down west of the Appalachians was in New Orleans. Milestone Number One of the Pontchartrain Railroad can still be seen, if you have a good guide, out on Elysian Fields Avenue, where, in September 1832, a steam engine shipped from England and named "Pontchartrain" puffed on its five-and-a-half-mile run out to the lake.

As railroads proliferated in the nineteenth century, lines converged on New Orleans from a number of directions and, as was true in Chicago, terminated in several different depots. A "union station" (imperfect as the union was, there still being half a dozen other stations) came to the Windy City late enough, in 1925. But such a wonder of interline cooperation and civic sensibleness was not achieved in the Crescent City (so called after the crescent-shaped bend in the Mississippi River) until 1952, just in time, New Orleanians joke, for the end of the passenger trains. The result in New Orleans was a modernistic rectangular building that for a few short years was a busy place served by some fine and finely named trains like the *Southern Belle* to Kansas City, the *Gulf Wind* to Jacksonville, the *Humming Bird* to Cincinnati, and of course the *Panama Limited*. Today they are gone, and the place is largely peopled by patrons of the bus lines who share the regrettably renamed Transportation Center with Amtrak.

Just as sad, few of these passengers, bus or train, seem to notice the splendid Diego Rivera–style murals that ring the spacious waiting room, depicting the panorama of Louisiana history from the conquistadores to the atomic age. There are four panels (the first two heavy on Frenchmen and nuns), and each rewards a long, concentrated stare. The one covering the antebellum years is, fittingly, the richest: the mural shows a fierce American eagle screeching down on a cringing British lion at the Battle of New Orleans in the War of 1812, along with depictions of Carnival, riverboat gamblers, boll weevils, yellow fever, and, yes, the railroad. The Four Horsemen gallop into the 1860s as the nation divides; a widow weeps over dying Confederate and Union soldiers; a wicked Yankee purloins the family silver. It is a fine performance, a better introduction to Louisiana than most tour guides could give, and something not to be found at the airport.

For train aficionados New Orleans boasts one other true distinction: it is terminus of the only two daily trains in America that are still equipped solely with passenger cars a full twenty to twenty-five years older than the government corporation that operates them. Amtrak aptly calls them its Heritage Fleet. The coaches, Pullmans, diners, and lounges on the *City of New Orleans* and the *Crescent* date from the 1940s and early 1950s, the twilight to be sure of the great day of passenger travel, but a grand enough twilight to have produced these last masterpieces of the car-builders' art. Since they have been refurbished, they bear the marks of the economies and tastes of the 1980s, but their identities are secure and unmistakable: great weight (107,000 pounds for a coach; 135,000 pounds for a diner; 127,000 pounds for a Pullman); great strength (steel frame and stainless steel construction); ample size (eighty-five feet long, ten feet wide, thirteen feet high). The coaches seat just forty-four people in the space where newer models put sixty-six and where a DC9 crams a hundred, and offer spacious lounges with porcelain fixtures, segregated for men and women. The Pullmans carry just twenty-two in ten roomettes (one bed each) and six double bedrooms (each with an upper and a lower, which convert into comfortable daytime seating). Each roomette has private facilities, a separate tap for circulating ice water, blue night lights, and a shoe compartment accessible from the corridor so that the porter can put a shine on while you sleep. In their youth many of these cars were pulled behind steam engines, and until their recent conversion to head-end electrical power they relied on steam generated from the locomotive for heat and hot water. They are the last of their kind, and when they are replaced with modern modular equipment, the last tangible

The levee still separates the Crescent City of New Orleans from the Mississippi River. The steamboats stacked high with cotton are long gone, but tankers and grain boats from afar still glide past today.

The Gulf, Mobile & Ohio's pocket streamliner *The Rebel* crosses Lake Pontchartrain en route to New Orleans in 1944.

link with the time when railroads vied for passengers and when the public found train travel both fashionable and efficient will have disappeared.

Bound for Atlanta, the Carolinas, Virginia, and the Northeast, the *Crescent* departs New Orleans in the early morning and for the next twenty-four hours travels the rails of another of the great trunk lines, the Southern Railway. Today part of the Norfolk Southern Corporation along with the old Norfolk & Western, the Southern was formed back in 1894 by financier J.P. Morgan out of the old Richmond & Danville system. From the beginning the line was closely associated with the New South movement, which from the 1880s to World War I proclaimed a gospel of sectional rejuvenation that called upon the states of the former Confederacy to put away the bitterness of defeat and to embrace new and, to an extent, Yankee ways on the road to true reunion and lasting prosperity. A "cotton mill crusade" brought the factories to the fields, farmers lessened their dependence on one-crop staple agriculture, and new railroads crisscrossed the region, binding it irrevocably to the North and to the nation.

The Southern's company logo long proclaimed that "The Southern Serves the South," and there was no prouder example of that service than the deluxe *Crescent Limited*. It began life on April 26, 1925, and it covered the 1,362 miles from New Orleans to New York in thirty-seven hours and fifty minutes. (Today's run is seven hours faster, over a route seventeen miles longer.) It was named in honor of the Crescent City of New Orleans, though the promotional brochure also portrayed its route — through Mobile, Montgomery, Atlanta, Charlotte, Washington, and Baltimore — as crescent-shaped, which it was. Three other railroads, the Louisville & Nashville, the Atlanta & West Point, and the Pennsylvania, cooperated to carry the *Crescent* over portions of its journey, but it was ever the Southern's own train. In the glory days, passage required payment of "a reasonable extra-fare" for extra amenities, which included a valet and a ladies' maid. Its Pullmans (named for distinguished citizens of the southern states, among them Henry W. Grady, prophet of the New South, and Joel Chandler Harris, author of the beloved Uncle Remus stories) were custom-painted in two tones of green and trimmed with genuine gold leaf. Its locomotives, also green, bore gold star-studded crescents on their cabs and cylinder boxes. One of these beauties can still be seen today at the Smithsonian Institution in Washington, D.C.

After World War II, the *Crescent* was elegantly re-equipped for the streamlined era, and it carried on with considerable élan under Southern management right up until 1979. This feat wins it the distinction of being the last truly great train in America to operate according to the standards of an older and better order of things: through the 1970s its patrons could still avail themselves of a Pullman master room with a shower, drink whiskey from glass glasses in a club car named "Crescent Moon," and, in a diner "with tablecloths, silverware, flowers, and those heavy plates," savor genuine southern specialties prepared by veteran Southern chef Louis Price who, as he claimed in the advertisement, cooked "just about everything on the train — even your breakfast muffins — just as I did when I started in 1941." Even the tradition of dedicated motive power lived on, with specially painted green and gold diesels that proudly bore the name of the train on their prow.

The *Crescent*'s route today varies somewhat from the original, running via Birmingham, Alabama, instead of through Mobile and Montgomery, but it is still a "Route of History, Scenery, and Romance" just as the timetable-copy crooned back in 1942. The distance from New Orleans to Washington on the present route is 1,155 miles, which the train covers in twenty-four hours, the half of it south of Atlanta in daylight. For the traveler keen to observe the expanse of the Deep South, there is no better way than this. It is a trip best taken in summer, partly because the days are long, but mostly because of the heat. Though the train is nicely air conditioned, stepping outside at the occasional station stop or standing at an open vestibule dutch door quickly reminds you of the pervasive, and oppressive, influence of climate on southern history. Temperatures that regularly reach the legendary 90°F. in the shade for three months of the year slow things down; man and beast just don't work as well when it's that hot. A perceptive Yankee friend who has lived in the South for forty years remarked to me on this trip that it was no wonder that for years the South was so underdeveloped or, more simply, so poor. "When the rest of the country is working twelve months and you're working just nine, well, it makes a difference." Too, it's real hard to catch up. Air conditioning has changed many ways down here and may be the single most important factor in the rise of the latest New South since 1945, but the South is still the nation's poor cousin. Old habits and the older pace linger on, and it is easiest to appreciate both their origins and their tenacity when you yourself swelter

As the drink list of its club lounge illustrated, the Louisville & Nashville linked the Ohio River at Cincinnati with bluegrass Kentucky horse farms, Tennessee's Parthenon, Alabama's cotton fields, and the Gulf Coast at New Orleans.

a bit under a southern sun. So get a Palm Beach suit and go in summer.

The heat combined with high humidity and usually abundant rainfall gives the southern landscape a lushness unique in America. Today it is largely tamed, but in earlier years the forest and swamps of this transmontane South were obstacles to be overcome as the land was brought under the plow. Unlike the coastal South, this region was wrested from nature and the Indians relatively late, in the 1830s and 1840s, and much of it was still frontier at the time of the Civil War. Here, hearty souls pioneered, a few with troops of slaves, most sweating right alongside their laborers, hewing out the farms and plantations of the Cotton Kingdom and fashioning in just a few short decades the timeless legend of the Old South. The names of the towns along the *Crescent*'s path tell some of the story. Slidell, Louisiana, refers to John Slidell, a Confederate diplomat whose interception on the high seas by the American navy nearly brought England into the Civil War on the southern side. Poplarville, Lumberton, and Richburg (named for a lumber baron) owe their names to one of Mississippi's and the South's most important modern crops: timber. In these latitudes you can grow a well-managed pine forest in about twenty years, and it is no wonder that the pulpwood car is the workhorse of southern freight trains and the cut trunks of pine trees a cargo even more common than cotton. Hattiesburg now boasts a state university but owes much to lumber, and so it goes, up through Laurel and Meridian.

Here in the lower South, where you can still get the strange feeling that the heat and the kudzu vine may just win out yet, other names on the land recall its earliest, unwritten history. Stations called Toomsuba, Tuscaloosa, and Talapoosa flash past the window. Displaced by a richer and more disciplined culture, the Indians of this region left their names on the sluggish streams that will forever drain it: Tallahatchie, Chickasawhay, Tombigbee, Black Warrior. A series of sleeping cars built for the streamlined *Crescent* carried the names of such rivers on their car end doors as well as on their letterboards. Walking through the train on the way to the diner was therefore a bit like a walk across the South, and added to the magic. What we call these states themselves, "Mississippi" and "Alabama," we owe to our aboriginal predecessors.

Alabama, "The Heart of Dixie," as the license plates say, introduces other themes. It was and is still richly agricultural, its famed Black Belt once the best cotton-producing land in the South and site of some of its finest plantation houses. But in Alabama a change occurs, and the train traveler can see it reflected in the station names: Bessemer, Birmingham, Irondale, Leeds. This was the first part of the South to be dubbed New, although in Alabama the gap in time between the New South and the Old one it supposedly supplanted was never very great. If proof was ever needed that railroads and heavy industry truly go together, then Birmingham, Alabama's chief city, is it. Named for the English iron and steel giant, it sprang up in the 1870s at a railroad junction in Jones Valley. The combined product of local ambitions and imported capital, it soon became the South's and one of the nation's great steel producers: Alabama's own Pittsburgh and Gary rolled into one. It demonstrated, so the boosters said, that the heavy-duty industrial revolution could happen happily in Dixie.

Though a mixed blessing, which brought to the South attitudes not truly native, the romance has been a lasting one. In the latest chapter, southern states keenly compete for Japanese and Yankee automobile plants. After the biggest deal yet was made in 1985 up in Tennessee, the state's governor, Lamar Alexander, wrote a series of wonderful ads that ran in all the big national press, as if to say this is how we do it down here. "Tennessee gets tomorrow's jobs," he declared, "because Tennesseans have yesterday's values." It is a beguiling idea to be sure, and a perennial problem in the South, where tradition and change have long kept uneasy company.

The next big city on the *Crescent*'s trip north is dedicated, if any place is, to the idea that material prosperity is good for southerners and to the conviction that they can acquire it with the best. Atlanta, from the 1880s when newspaperman Henry W. Grady so christened it, right down to the present, has been the capital of the New South. The *Crescent* leaves here at about 7:30 P.M., thus providing fast overnight service to the Northeast. Long famous because Sherman burned it in 1864 and Margaret Mitchell wrote about it in 1936, Atlanta is also the home of Coca-Cola, of the world's first revolving-top Hyatt hotel, of an airport that is the envy of most other cities, and of a fancy new subway system. Alas, it has just two daily passenger trains (one north, one south), and they no longer stop downtown. They are well patronized, though: for the run north to Washington and New York additional coaches, Pullmans, and mail cars are added here. Indeed, the scene at pleasant old suburban Peachtree Street Station is reminiscent of older times, with

The streamliner *City of Miami*, seen here in Alabama in 1947, connected Chicago and the Midwest with the Florida resorts. Its companion train, the *South Wind*, ran on alternate days.

a couple of hundred passengers crowding the waiting room and the platform, wagons piled high with checked baggage, and carmen servicing a long train about to set out on a fast run. The elegant Southern dining and club cars are no more, and the ladies in white gloves and the gentlemen in white suits will no longer be found among the passengers, but an air unquestionably lingers that is rich in old southern associations. Standing sentinel over this scene (although now largely ignored) is a handsome statue in a well-kept courtyard adjacent to the station. He is Samuel Spencer, 1847–1916: "A Georgian, A Confederate Soldier, and First President of the Southern Railway." The statue was erected by the employees and rededicated on July 3, 1970. As the old slogan said: "The Southern Serves the South."

North from Atlanta in twilight and darkness, the *Crescent* plies the Piedmont, that region of rich farms, textile mills, and furniture factories between tidewater and the mountains. This is an eastern and an older South. Georgia was named for George II in the eighteenth century, the Carolinas for the Stuart Charleses in the seventeenth, Virginia for the Tudor Elizabeth, the Virgin Queen, in the sixteenth, which is as far back as English America goes. As night falls, you are still in Georgia somewhere near Flowery Branch where no trains stop anymore. Your eye and mind behold a classic image of this place and the time it encompasses: a burned-down house with only two brick chimneys left standing as if Sherman had just passed through, and next door a modern rancher right out of the catalog, with children splashing in the pool. The train will pass through Charlotte, North Carolina, at about one o'clock in the morning and six hours after that Charlottesville, Virginia, both named for Charlotte, consort of George III and the last queen of America. Nine o'clock will bring the Potomac River and the Federal City, and with them the end of the South — and the Southern.

More than most national capitals (which are usually cities in their own right, with reasons for being other than politics), Washington, D.C., is a political place. Though recently polished up to a luster befitting a great power, it is not unlike a small university or company town, where there is one primary employer, one institutional focus of civic attention, and, like it or not, one overpowering image held up to the outer world. For the rest of America over the last half-century or so, Washington in addition to being a splendid symbol of national power has become more mundanely the dispenser of good things or (if the administration happens to be a conservative one) the allocator of deprivations. It is the place where public servants, private interests, and assorted parasites tussle over power, favor, and influence — all the stuff of politics in a free society. The "bottom line," as they say, is that there is a lot of public and private money in Washington these days, and it makes for a lot of action.

While not exactly at the center of it, Amtrak (the National Railroad Passenger Corporation, as it is described in the legislation) is an agency of the federal government with offices in Washington not far from Union Station, which was so woefully degraded into a visitors' center during the Bicentennial but is now being returned to its intended purpose as a grand portal to a grand city. Established in 1971, Amtrak has by now managed to establish a solid enough record of rebuilding a modest rail passenger network and seems assured of survival in the federal budget. It has been around long enough to have become something of a legislative habit on Capitol Hill, and its trains pass through so many congressional districts that its wholesale elimination would be a very difficult political act. Its subsidy is hardly munificent by Washington standards; it is positively niggardly by the standards of European and Japanese nationalized rail systems and is far less than is required to do the job properly.

Amtrak's intractable problem of living on inadequate short-term budgets can be observed most clearly in what was once the very pinnacle of the rail travel experience: the dining car. Here today you will find generally pleasant employees trying hard, but with not a lot to work with. Even in the glory days, dining cars lost thousands of dollars for the railroads, but the superior standard of service then was viewed as invaluable public relations, and the deficits were paid for with freight. So, too, the diners lost money for Amtrak (which, alas, has no money-making freight), until budget-cutters in the early 1980s found it politically uncomfortable to continue subsidizing dining cars equipped with china and adequate staffs while contemplating cutting the appropriation for food stamps. It is certainly a debatable point, but the diners lost. As a result, generally good food is served on plastic plates with paper napkins and disposable tablecloths; forty-eight-seat cars meant to be staffed by six waiters and a steward are run with two or three waiters and no steward. Who's to blame? If you think it's a combination of too little money and the declining taste of a public that has grown used to fast food and has just about forgotten how to travel anyway, you will be close to the sad truth.

In the 1920s the *Panama Limited* boasted Pullman luxuries and a fast overnight schedule from Chicago to New Orleans.

Charged to live within their means, Amtrak's administrators stretch a little a very long way. It is not an easy job in a country where since the 1950s vast public subsidy has gone to highways and airways while the rails languished, and where the public (except for commuters in the largest cities) have long since gotten out of the habit of riding the train. Today Amtrak carries a lot of people, though still a relatively small portion of total intercity travelers, something that is not likely to change greatly in an uncrowded country of vast distances whose citizens crave speed and convenience above all things. Still, Amtrak trains move passengers over the rails with reasonable dispatch and in considerable comfort. If the agency could somehow be relieved of the yearly budget fights that prevent effective long-range capital planning, it would be assured of a bright future.

So Amtrak's executives sit today in offices in the very shadow of the United States Capitol, which yearly decides their future: "A helluva way to run a railroad," as the old saying goes. Yet run it does, and Washington, D.C., its headquarters and a place rich in historical associations, is a fitting place to begin our final trunk line journey: the Chesapeake & Ohio, whose name so aptly describes its territory. Actually our third capital (until 1800 the seat of government was first in New York then in Philadelphia), Washington was named for George Washington, who also helped select the site for his namesake city along the Potomac River. Commander of the Continental forces in the war against the British and first president of the United States, Washington was the first of our Founding Fathers in every way: "First in war, first in peace, first in the hearts of his countrymen," as Richard Henry Lee everlastingly put it in his eulogy the day after Christmas 1799. For Americans and foreigners ever since, Washington has been one of those protean figures about whom the myth and the man are happily confused. Nor for most people does the confusion much matter. In Washington the city, his is a pervasive symbolic presence: the obelisk of his monument dominates the District's European-like low-level skyline; countless likenesses on canvas or in marble and bronze remind us of him; his face bedecks every almighty dollar bill churned out at the Bureau of Printing and Engraving; and a few miles away his lovely family seat, Mount Vernon, looks down across sweeping lawns to the broad Potomac.

For nearly forty years, the premier train of the Chesapeake & Ohio Railway, which joined the tidal Potomac with the westward-flowing Ohio, also bore the name of America's

first president, whose stern likeness, as portrayed by Gilbert Stuart, proudly rode its observation car railing. No words, just a painting, it was probably the loveliest, most understated drumhead sign ever to grace an American passenger train: the perfect marriage of commerce and culture. If George Washington was the nation's first Founding Father, he was also the most revered native son in a state where there were many. Virginia long and rightly thought of itself as the mother of presidents: four of our first five were born there. Washington, of course, was the first, and the train that carried his name over the C&O had about it, beginning to end, a distinctly gracious Virginia air. It debuted on April 24, 1932, to mark (two months late) the 200th anniversary of Washington's birth, and it topped the C&O's timetable right up to May 1, 1971, when Amtrak, which kept the route, sadly dropped the name. Everything about it carefully cultivated the remembered stateliness of

There had been a spa for the well-to-do at White Sulphur Springs, West Virginia, since antebellum times, but only after the Chesapeake & Ohio Railway built the Greenbrier Hotel there in 1913 on an estate of 6,000 acres did it become the supreme monument to the gentility of the Old South.

colonial Virginia and the antebellum South. Dining cars named "Michie's Tavern," "Gadsby's Tavern," and "Raleigh Tavern" served up a $1.25 Mount Vernon Dinner featuring Chesapeake Bay seafood in a setting of off-white wood paneling, carriage lamps, and Duncan Phyfe chairs. The Pullmans, which carried the train's and not the railroad's name on the letterboards, themselves carried names connected with Washington's exploits: "First Citizen" for the man himself, "Baron Rochambeau" after the French connection without which the Revolutionary War might well have had a different outcome. The twin Pullman observation cars "Commander-in-Chief" and "American Revolution" offered passengers a serene library lounge with prints of Emanuel Leutze's *Washington Crossing the Delaware* and *The Signing of the Declaration of Independence* and, in an archway niche, a bust of the Founding Father presented to the C&O by the Washington Bicentennial Commission.

For many of the first-class passengers (the train also carried unprecedentedly luxurious coaches dubbed Imperial Salon Cars, featuring carpeting and 2-1 seating), such soft-spoken southern elegance was only prelude to the palatial Greenbrier Hotel at White Sulphur Springs, West Virginia, which the C&O built in 1913 on the site of the original historic health spa once patronized by the likes of Robert E. Lee. With Lucullan standards of food and service and 6,000 acres of preserved mountain fastness, it became in the 1920s a mecca, fully equal to the Flagler resorts in Florida, for the nation's social and business elite — all, it might be added, amid one of the most drearily impoverished regions of the country. As late as the 1960s, customers still came from New York and the Midwest on the Pullmans of *The George* and the C&O's other name trains: the *Sportsman*, the *Resort Special*, and the *F.F.V.*, which stood either for "First Families of Virginia" or for "Fast Flying Virginian" (the railroad never would say which). In fact, the green and white station at White Sulphur Springs is still an Amtrak stop, and the hotel will still send a limousine down to fetch you.

The C&O was eminently clear, however, when it came to declaring its own corporate ancestry. With some typographical flourish its timetables and dining car menus proclaimed it to be "George Washington's Railroad," which was not completely the public relations sleight of hand it seemed on the surface: George Washington died in 1799, years before railroads made their American debut. The C&O was legitimately descended, as the timetables also

HOW TO AVOID DELAYS & ACCIDENTS!

NEW YORK CENTRAL & HUDSON RIVER R.R.
THE ONLY FOUR-TRACK RAILROAD IN THE WORLD

said, from a company founded by George Washington in 1785, just two years after the signing of the Peace of Paris, which confirmed the colonists' battlefield victory and ended Washington's active career as a military hero. Other exploits lay ahead for Washington, leading ultimately to his election to the presidency of the infant United States of America in 1792. In the years in between, private as well as public matters occupied him, chief among them tending to his extensive landholdings in the region that later became West Virginia, and promoting transportation development between that western wilderness and the Virginia Tidewater, where his inherited holdings were also substantial. The Chesapeake & Ohio Canal, whose remnants are preserved today between Georgetown and Harpers Ferry, was one of his pet projects. The canal was to connect the Potomac and Monongahela watersheds and so funnel western commerce to the sea via Virginia. After the Hudson–Mohawk corridor in New York State, this was the easiest natural transportation route across the Appalachians. But by the time the C&O Canal crested the mountains at Cumberland, Maryland, in the 1850s, it was eight years behind the Baltimore & Ohio Railroad, and the waterway's ultimate redundancy was assured.

Farther to the south, a more difficult route through the mountain barrier lay long the James–Kanawha corridor, extraordinarily rugged terrain first spied out by English-

In the 1870s and 1880s the New York Central boasted of a four-track mainline to allay public fears about the safety of railroad travel. A century later, passenger trains are still the safest way to travel.

man Robert Fallam in 1671, who recorded that it was "a pleasing tho' dreadful sight to see mountains and Hills as if piled one upon the other." It was over a century later that George Washington himself inspected the region, which much to his disappointment offered no good all-Virginia alternative to the transmontane corridor that led up the Potomac to Pennsylvania. And it was yet another century before the rails of the C&O penetrated the thousand-foot-deep New River Gorge to connect the old Virginia Central with the Ohio via the Greenbrier River, the Kanawha, and the Teays Valley. To ride this line across the Virginias today, as you still can in daylight, is to be confirmed in the judgment of those earlier visitors who found all about them such "a pleasing tho' dreadful sight."

The C&O's *George Washington* traditionally provided fast overnight service from Washington (there was also a connecting section that came up from Newport News and Richmond) to Cincinnati and Louisville, both on the Ohio, with through cars for Chicago, which was reached early the next afternoon. This schedule meant a cocktail-time departure from Washington's Union Station, through the tunnel under the Capitol, across the Potomac to Alexandria, and, if the weather and season were right, a fine sunset-lit dinner as the train passed across historic northern Virginia to Charlottesville, where the Richmond cars swelled the train. From Charlottesville, the train climbed the Blue Ridge Mountains in darkness up to Rockfish Gap and Afton Tunnel, then screeched downgrade in a cloud of brakeshoe smoke to a quick stop at Waynesboro, where the C&O shared a unique bilevel station with the Norfolk & Western, and then roared out across the beautiful Shenandoah — the Valley of Virginia.

Today's Amtrak schedule more closely approximates the carding of the old *Sportsman*, thus forfeiting the poignant ride at twilight through Manassas and across so many Civil War battlegrounds, but it thereby gains daylight for the passage through the New River Gorge in West Virginia. Less fortunate is the loss under Amtrak of the fine old name, *George Washington*. Now the train is called, rather less strikingly, the *Cardinal*, presumably after Virginia's state bird. And, of course, it is shorn of all of its old C&O/Virginia distinctiveness. Still it remains a very pleasant train, equipped with solid cars from the 1940s and 1950s, and run on an unhurried schedule through some of the finest scenery in America.

For years, passengers on the *George Washington* were

greeted at the C&O's Main Street Station in Charlottesville, Virginia, by tasteful trackside signs announcing that this was the home of Thomas Jefferson's Monticello. It was as if, after both were long dead, these two most famous of the Founding Fathers still saluted each other with the daily arrival of the *George Washington* in Thomas Jefferson's town. Today from the train window of the *Cardinal* you can catch a quick glimpse of Jefferson's arcaded "academical village," the University of Virginia, although this best of American campuses more than repays a special visit. And a stop is mandatory in order to see Jefferson's true masterpiece, Monticello, without a doubt the finest house in America, atop its 867-foot mountain with its commanding views of the Piedmont to the east and the Blue Ridge Mountains to the west. From here Thomas Jefferson traveled to Philadelphia to write the Declaration of Independence, to serve as Minister to France, as George Washington's first secretary of state, and from 1801 to 1809 as president of the new nation. George Washington himself was a visitor here (as was Jefferson at Mount Vernon): both Virginians treasured time spent in the country away from public affairs.

The scenery is deceptive, for most of it overlies huge deposits of coal. West Virginia's chief natural resource, coal not surprisingly found its way onto the official state seal in the shape of a miner displaying his tools. Coal also lends some irony to the official state motto: *Montani semper liberi* (Mountaineers are always free). For if ever a state was colonized and not free, it was this one, and coal was a chief cause. Whether in Silesia, northern Japan, Wales, or West Virginia, coal has commonly been judged more a curse than a blessing on the land that yielded it. An industry beholden to distant markets, coal-mining extracted much from those whose lives it touched. In West Virginia, the boom-and-bust nature of the business drew in a larger population than the state's other economic resources could ever support, so that, as one observer put it, the state was forever "hooked on coal," like an addict getting in deeper all the time. In the absence of an economically healthy home market, the state's resources, coal chief among them, sped away to industrial centers in the North and Midwest on the long black trains of the C&O, which you can still see in abundance rumbling past the pristine gates of the Greenbrier. Particularly in southern West Virginia, the coal lay in rugged areas never attractive to agriculture; therefore, when the coal operators did arrive after the Civil War, they built,

The rotunda and colonnade of the University of Virginia in Charlottesville were the centerpieces of Thomas Jefferson's "academical village." You can still catch a glimpse of them from the passing train.

of necessity (and for better or for worse, usually for worse), the company towns and stores that became a complete social environment for the miners and miners' families who thereby became their captives.

The sad record of mine disasters and of bloody battles between mine operators and union organizers reveals an especially bitter history behind the beauty of the region's mountains and valleys. A 1913 confrontation between the owners and the United Mine Workers around Cabin Creek and Paint Creek in the Kanawha field east of Charleston pitted the eighty-three-year-old legendary organizer Mary "Mother Jones" Harris against the guardians of good order who fitted out an armored train to protect their strikebreakers. On a recent trip through Thurmond, West Virginia, the veteran train conductor described the place as a big, roaring town in the 1930s when, it was said, more money passed through in coal than could be had in Richmond and Cincinnati combined. As he spoke, the train passed movie actors and extras milling about during the filming of *Matewan Story* (even though Matewan is actually located to the south, on the Norfolk & Western). It was the

1920 Matewan Massacre, another bloody duel between owners and miners, that left, after the smoke cleared, ten people dead.

The *Cardinal* gives you good steady exposure to this gloomy place, past Hawk's Nest, Gauley, Mount Carbon, and Cabin Creek. Today as the train reaches the western end of the New River Gorge near Hawk's Nest, it passes 856 feet below the New River Gorge Bridge, the world's longest single-arch span bridge. It is an impressive sight, but one that in West Virginia is as much a reminder of man's and technology's frailties as of their triumphs. It was not far from here that the Hawk's Nest Tunnel was bored under Gauley Mountain in the 1930s, bringing New River water to a new hydroelectric station — and death by silicosis to 476 of the

"Home of Monticello," the sign said on the station platform in Charlottesville, Virginia. Of all the houses of American presidents, none more precisely reflected the character of its master than Thomas Jefferson's beloved Monticello. Begun in 1769 and not truly finished even at his death fifty-seven years later, the house and grounds were his chief private joy.

men who dug it. And it was about halfway between the New River bridge and Matewan, site of the 1920 massacre, that on February 26, 1972, a dam made from mine refuse burst on Buffalo Creek, releasing 135 million gallons of water into the winding hollow below and killing 125 people.

It is a melancholy journey, this train ride across the Virginias, reminding the traveler as it does of the considerable gulf separating the pretentious elegance of the Greenbrier from the reality of the coal fields nearby. It is also a journey that reminds the traveler of the connection between that long-lost prerailway age and the times that followed. It links Virginia, whose glory was so assuredly of the eighteenth century, with the western interior of America, whose history would be played out only in the nineteenth century. Overnight, you will have covered a hundred years. The signs were there all along. George Washington — hero of the first successful colonial revolution and the father of his country — was also a speculator in western lands and a promoter of transportation development in the region where one day a fine train would proudly carry his name and portrait. Thomas Jefferson — diplomat, author, architect — was also a farmer and landholder and, like Washington, a man who saw that the American future lay westward beyond his own beloved native Virginia, and early in his presidency he took the bold step that made that future a certainty. When the opportunity suddenly arose in 1803, Jefferson as president agreed to the purchase from Napoleon of the whole Louisiana Territory, a tract of 828,000 square miles reaching from the Mississippi to the Rocky Mountains and from Canada to the Gulf of Mexico. Under his direction Meriwether Lewis (his nephew) and William Clark undertook their epic exploration of this vast expanse all the way to the Pacific Ocean, and in so doing rendered the United States henceforth a continental nation. (Monticello still contains relics from the expedition.) This new western nation was destined to become something rather different from the fledgling republic wrought by the Founding Fathers from a string of seaboard colonies bound to the Atlantic world. Among other things, it would depend heavily on railroads both for its ultimate economic development and for its immediate links to older eastern centers of power. These railroads, the great transcontinentals, were themselves confirmation of Washington's and Jefferson's visions of a vast land neither ever saw.

Victorian gingerbread graces the
station at Paoli on the mainline of
the Pennsylvania Railroad. As rivers
once did, the railroads shaped and
gave names to the human landscape
around them. The Pennsylvania
Railroad's mainline runs west from
Philadelphia through posh suburbs
that to this day are called the
Mainline.

Misty rain provides atmosphere for the start of a night journey on the *River Cities* down the Mississippi from St. Louis to Memphis and New Orleans.

One of the oldest lines in America, the Pennsylvania Railroad (now Conrail) west from Philadelphia to Pittsburgh journeys through a long-domesticated landscape. Here the railroad embankment bridges the flood plain and playing fields of Downingtown, Pennsylvania.

In central Pennsylvania, Amish laundry dries in front of a clerestory coach belonging to the Strasburg Railroad, the oldest line in America operating under its original charter (signed in 1832).

The pastoral and the industrial
alternate in the train window
between Philadelphia and Pittsburgh, Pennsylvania. In Coastville,
the train crosses a river valley occupied by an early steel mill.

An industrial switcher belches
upgrade to the main trunk line used
by all passenger trains traveling
east from Chicago. The grain elevators and twin lift bridge (right) over
the Calumet River are now
abandoned.

Spur lines, built to service local industries, are little used today, their duties now performed by trucks. In New York State, a little-used spur crosses the once-bustling Erie Canal, which opened the interior to commerce in the 1830s but was soon superseded by the railroad.

Passengers on the steam trains of
the Strasburg Railroad in Pennsylvania ride through rich farmland
cultivated in the time-honored
tradition.

Viewed from the now abandoned
station at Gary, Indiana, this fabri-
cated steel and linear landscape
long symbolized America's industrial prowess.

Railroads built 150 years ago with human and animal muscle are maintained today with precision machines and little labor. Conrail equipment tests track on the heavy grades in the Allegheny Mountains.

Leisure craft and the *International
Limited* share the shoreline of Lake
Michigan. Michigan City, Indiana, is
a harbor for yachtsmen and headquarters for the Chicago, South-
shore & South Bend Railroad.

In central Pennsylvania, a train
rumbles past old competitors, now
all tired out.

Following pages: One of just four
border crossings used by passenger
trains between the United States
and Canada, the Whirlpool Bridge
at Niagara Falls, 780 feet long and
226 feet above the Niagara River, is
surely one of the most spectacular
border crossings anywhere in the
world. Every day the *Maple Leaf*,
en route from Toronto to New York,
pauses briefly in the middle, at the
border.

Trestles and buttresses carry the
rails over the industry-rich Cuya-
hoga Valley at Cleveland, Ohio, on
the shore of Lake Erie.

The romantic ideal proclaimed in
name and form by the sign at this
commuter station contrasts with
the utilitarian snout of the morning
train to Chicago.

"Player with railroads" was one of the ways poet Carl Sandburg described Chicago. In the 1850s the powerful Illinois Central (IC) preempted much of the city's lakefront for station and yards, and by the end of the century the city boasted half a dozen major stations and hundreds of passenger trains to every point of the compass. Today the railroads are much diminished in Chicago as elsewhere, but the remnant of the IC's yards, shown here along South Michigan Avenue, is a reminder of the time when this was the greatest railroad town of all.

A busy grade crossing at Elmhurst, a western suburb of Chicago. Chicago commuters travel in double-decked gallery cars, which were built in the 1950s and 1960s and enjoy right-of-way over automobiles and bicycles.

Left: The waiting room at Chicago's Union Station is all that remains of the city's six passenger terminals from the great age of travel (Illinois Central Station, Grand Central, LaSalle Street, Dearborn, North-western, and Union). Modeled after the Baths of Carcalla in Rome, it opened in 1925, the heyday of the passenger train. Thousands (mostly commuters) still use it today.

Above: A generous wooden bench at Chicago's Union Station continues to provide rest and convenience for weary families. Such hospitality contrasts sharply with the austere plastic buckets that provide only seating in airports and contemporary railroad stations.

THE TRANS-CONTINENTALS

"Rocky" the mountain goat and the Blackfoot Indians were long identified with the Great Northern, as seen on the cover of this dining-car menu from 1942. Inside, a whole Pacific Ocean jumbo crab was offered for 60 cents (on mainline trains, eastbound).

The transcontinental railroads traversed great distances and overcame great natural obstacles of which the Continental Divide in the Rocky Mountains was the greatest. Even the lowest rail crossing (on the Great Northern at Marias Pass in Montana) carried trains to more than 5,200 feet in elevation, where up to 200 inches of snow could fall in winter.

The vision of Thomas Jefferson and the exploits of Meriwether Lewis and William Clark, his explorers, antedated the transcontinental railroads by over six decades. But thanks to a practice once common in the heyday of the American passenger train and sustained into the 1950s, the presence both of the president and of the expedition daily rode the Northern Pacific's Chicago–Seattle *North Coast Limited*, on buffet-lounge cars named "Lewis and Clark's Traveller's Rest," after the explorers' campsite in Montana near where the Northern Pacific would one day run. Adorned with portraits of the two pathfinders after the Charles Wilson Peale originals and with murals depicting their meeting with Sacagawea and their route to the Pacific, the cars evoked that special sense of simultaneous movement through time and space that is peculiar to train travel.

The names were more than just a nice touch; they reflected the history of the land they crossed, as did the train that ran on the other, more northerly route between Chicago and the Pacific Northwest: Great Northern's *Empire Builder*. The name survives to this day in Amtrak's timetable, and the train still plies every day across the far northern edge of the country. It is an important name, referring to both a particular and much-revered personage and to a certain indisputable spirit of the West. For if ever a region inspired thinking in imperial terms, it was the trans-Mississippi West, which Thomas Jefferson's Louisiana Purchase first made American and thus part of what he himself called "an empire for liberty." Jefferson foresaw an orderly step-by-step process whereby in the United States new territories would first establish a republican form of government, then be admitted to national representation, and finally achieve statehood on terms of full equality with much older eastern commonwealths. It was a process of state-making that reconciled the ancient conflict between liberty and empire, and every western state is a product of it.

The transcontinental railroads — which in the thirty years after the Civil War crossed Jefferson's "Louisiana," crested the Rockies and high deserts, and reached the Pacific — played a large part in this story of western settlement. It was a story to which, beginning in the 1930s, Hollywood fondly attached the word *epic* — and came very close to the truth. The very names of these railroads suggested heroic scale, romantic destination and, yes, imperial ambition: Union Pacific, Southern Pacific, Santa Fe, Northern Pacific, Great Northern. Of them all, the Great Northern (route of the *Empire Builder*) was the last finished and the least in keeping with the swashbuckling image of the Old West. That its premier train carried the truly imperial name (and successfully bequeathed it to a nationalized passenger service run by civil servants in Washington, D.C.) is the best evidence of the ties between a railroad and a truer and more lasting kind of empire.

The empire builder in question was not Jefferson but James Jerome Hill, a Canadian-born entrepreneur who punched through the Great Northern's mainline from St. Paul, Minnesota, to the salt water of Puget Sound in the late 1880s and early 1890s. Not finished until 1893, the Great Northern was the last of the great transcontinentals, and never falling into receivership in the perilous years to come, it was also the soundest. It was unique in one other respect, which also reveals something important about the empire Hill built. The Great Northern was built without the munificent subsidy of federal land grants, which bestowed on the other western lines acreages equivalent to some entire eastern states. Consequently, the Great Northern paid as it went because it had to, and a map of its route across the northern tier depicts how. Branches sprouted from the well-built mainline, penetrating the wheat country and tying it to eastern markets. Across North Dakota, before the coming of the hard-surface highway, trains reached out to scores of little towns on what was one of America's last-settled frontiers: Hannah, Walhalla, Dunseith, Antler, Sherwood, Crosby. The form was simple and classic. A local chugged off the mainline, stopping every five to ten miles to service the little white depots and towering grain elevators that dot these prairies. The train would overnight at the end of the branch, and next morning head back again — at harvest time trailing long lines of red boxcars filled with the wheat that in this part of the world is wealth. Into the late 1950s some of these locals still carried an ancient combination mail-express-passenger car in lieu of a caboose, so keeping alive for a little while the now vanished "mixed train." It was an empire of wheat and cattle and farmers, of Norwegians, Swedes, and Germans whose debt to Hill, the empire builder, was large and lasting. Held in an esteem that the more buccaneering moguls of the other transcontinentals might well have envied, Hill exemplified terrific

James Jerome Hill, the "Empire Builder," forged his Great Northern Railway between St. Paul and Seattle in the 1880s and 1890s without federal land grants. Into the 1970s, Hill's portrait hung in the dining cars of the train named after him: the *Empire Builder*.

talent and ambition put to the service of the private and the public interest. In the wide-open world of Gilded Age capitalism where the winnings could be handsome (Hill's were: he left an estate of $53 million, much to the Church, and a fine collection of modern French art), Hill put in more than he took out and was revered by the plain people of the Northwest because he deserved it.

Hill's Great Northern was the best of the transcontinentals, and it best illustrates the central strategic fact that distinguishes these roads from all others. Unlike older eastern lines that were built to connect existing cities and to tap markets any capitalist could see, the transcontinentals connected no population centers, but rather were built to create them. It was the "supply side" in action long before there was a fancy theory by that name: a game only for real gamblers with cunning, vision, and faith enough to foresee settlement where none was and where much conventional wisdom said none was likely to be. Better than any of the others, Hill was the one who followed through on this faith. As the Great Northern went west, its agents recruited farmers or would-be farmers to settle the potentially rich lands along its tracks, and then worked with them to master the High Plains and to improve their land and farming practices. Hill himself was fascinated with cattle and wheat. He imported Angus from Scotland and gave away seven thousand head of pure-bred breeding stock. He established an agronomy department at the Great Northern and made a policy of distributing yearly three boxcars full of the best seed grains to improve yields and, in the natural course of things, the Great Northern's business, too.

Such attentiveness to current prosperity and future markets was matched by the quality of the line itself, which was surveyed and constructed with extraordinary care. The engineering was superior, with grades not exceeding one percent. At Marias Pass in the Montana Rockies, the Great Northern achieved the lowest-level crossing of the Continental Divide of any of the transcontinentals, a mere 5,200 feet above sea level. This was the legendary "lost pass" that the Indians had described to (but had failed to find for) Meriwether Lewis in 1805. Hill gave renowned engineer John F. Stevens the job of locating it, which he did in the winter of 1889. With its discovery, Hill's Great Northern finished the work that Jefferson's men had begun in that long-lost prerailway age. The Great Northern itself was finished on January 6, 1893, nearly a quarter-century after the first transcontinental, the Union Pacific/Central Pacific, met at the famous union at Promontory Summit, Utah, complete with golden spikes and polished laurel wood tie. Ever mindful of substance over display, Hill called for nothing special to mark the event: he himself was not present, and the last spike on the Great Northern was a plain iron one.

It is significant that only the Great Northern in years hence chose to preserve the memory of its builder in its corporate image. "Route of the Empire Builder," its timetables proclaimed into the 1960s, in reference to its premier Chicago–Seattle passenger train. Even in the 1970s and 1980s the name endured, though its meaning no doubt was something of a mystery to novice rail travelers poorly versed in regional history. Happily, Amtrak has now restored descriptive route maps that explain to the curious exactly who this empire builder was. But it was with the previous generation's *Empire Builder* that Hill's presence was evoked most powerfully. This matched set of five beautiful streamliners debuted in 1955, and in their Pullman green, Omaha orange, and gold-striped livery they were the most visually striking trains of this, the closing chapter of grand railroad passenger service in America.

These streamliners offered both coach and Pullman service and featured four glass-topped vista-domes (dubbed "Great Domes") apiece, three for coach passengers and one full-length dome with lower-level cocktail lounge for the carriage trade in the Pullmans. Interiors dazzled with Northwest Coast Indian motifs and the pastels of prairie and mountain. A unique coffee-shop lounge, the "Ranch Car," offered economy-priced meals and a lounge for coach passengers amid a western setting of pinto leather chairs, branding irons, peeled pole timbers, and oak-paneled walls. The Great Northern's own brand, the G Bar N, was prominently affixed to an overhead timber and was officially registered with the Montana Livestock Association. In the classically appointed dining cars, carved-glass partitions depicted Northwest forests and Dakota prairies; spotless linen was bedecked with seven-piece place settings and silver water pitchers; the menu offered lamb chops, lobster, roast beef, and pike. In the morning, the demitasse while you ordered came compliments of the steward. In the evening, toasted crackers with Kaukauna Klub cheese was obligatory. And from over the buffet in the center of the car, a lowering likeness of the old one-eyed Jim Hill himself looked on, as if to leave no doubt that this was his train, his railroad, his empire.

Today it requires some historical imagination to recover

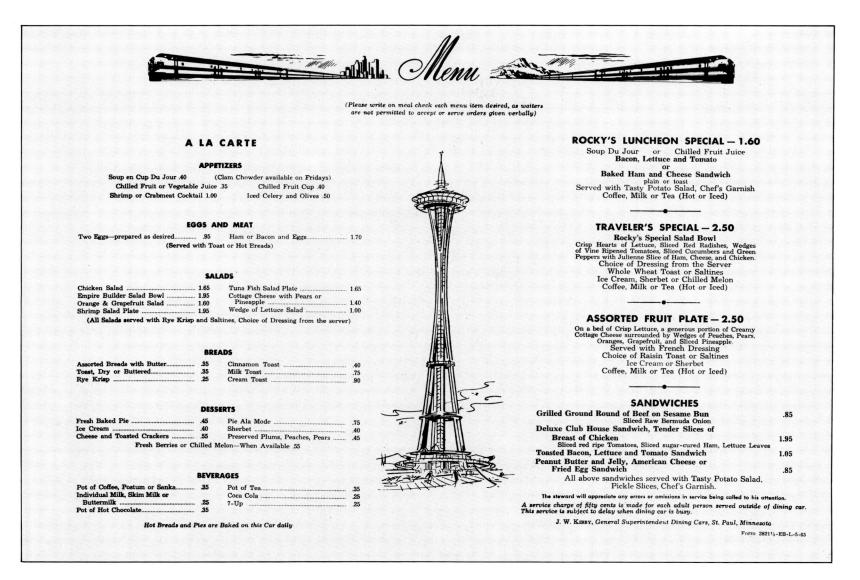

Aboard the *Empire Builder* in the 1960s, luncheon was served on heavy Syracuse china, with silver plate, white linen, and fresh flowers.

these older meanings. Amtrak is no respecter of original routings, and the westbound *Empire Builder* doesn't even reach the rails of the old Great Northern until Fargo, North Dakota, more than six hundred miles from Chicago. And the train consists of Amtrak-issue bilevel cars, identical to those on every other train west of Chicago. The first leg of the journey, to the Twin Cities, once over the Burlington Route's splendid Mississippi River line, now follows the Soo Line (late the bankrupt Milwaukee Road) through Milwaukee and central Wisconsin. It is a pleasant enough ride. Milwaukee offers a last glimpse of the remains of the old urban industrial landscape before the farming landscape that stretches westward for the next thousand miles. It is a city where immigrant populations made and moved things: old signs proclaim "Milwaukee Valve Company," "Wisconsin Cold Storage Company," "Catholic Knights Insurance"; ore boats ride high at harbor quays. To the northwest, marshes and woodlands separate station stops like Columbus, Portage (a lot of which was once done in this part of the world), La Crosse. At Wisconsin Dells, a tourist mecca and visual throwback to the 1950s, flashing neon announces "shirt shack," "mocassins," and, naturally, cheese. From La Crosse the line clings to the west bank of the Mississippi, not as scenic as the Burlington's route farther south, but a fine vantage nonetheless on the upper reaches of America's greatest river. In summer it is possible to catch a glimpse here of the steamboat *Delta Queen*, last of the overnight wooden stern-wheelers on the continent — or more likely one of the many long tows of bulk cargo that ply this vast river system.

After dinner, the *Empire Builder* reaches the Twin Cities of St. Paul and Minneapolis, each of which once had its own grand station. The changeover from Burlington to Great Northern crews and locomotives always came at St. Paul (the Hill Mansion still stands in St. Paul, and is now preserved by the Minnesota Historical Society); Minneapolis, the great flour-milling center across the river, was reached half an hour later. St. Paul had a union station, shared by several railroads, but in Minneapolis the Great Northern had its very own, where expectant crowds gathered beneath handsome murals depicting Lewis and Clark's western explorations, while waiting upon the *Empire Builder* and the Great Northern's lesser trains: the *Winnipeg Limited*, the *Gopher*, the *Badger*, the *Red River*, the *Dakotan*. Today the murals, the station, most of the crowds, and all the trains except the *Empire Builder* are gone. But as Amtrak #7 nightly departs St. Paul for the West, it keeps alive something of the spirit of its nobler predecessors and holds open to the modern rail passenger this, the capital city of Jim Hill's empire.

By the wee hours the train is on the rich prairie land of the Red River Valley, which it follows due north from Fargo, North Dakota, to Grand Forks, home of the "Fighting Sioux of North Dakota U." and, west of town, a large Strategic Air Command base. A picturesque college town of elm trees and old houses, Grand Forks until recently had a conveniently located railroad station downtown just east of the river. To reach the station, however, passenger trains had to complete a long backing operation to get on and off the east–west mainline. This had charm but took time and thus money, and is therefore no longer tolerated. A new station now sits forlornly west of town, about as conveniently located as the airport.

West to Minot the train is at sea in prairie broken a century ago by pioneers who made their first houses out of it. Dawn here reveals an immense land open to the horizon, punctuated by farmyard lights and shelter belts of box elder and cottonwood, most planted by those first settlers and now passing away themselves.

It was from the little towns along here, with their grain elevators and green-trimmed brick or white clapboard depots, that Hill thrust out his branches north and west to

Great Northern's *Empire Builder* pauses at Willmar, Minnesota, in the 1930s, bound from Chicago to Puget Sound.

bring back the wheat. At Devils Lake in a wet year there is water in the lake and waterfowl. And always there is the stately brick hotel next to the station. Fifty-eight miles farther on at Rugby you find yourself at the geographical center of the North American continent, a distinction so marked by an obelisk south of the tracks on parallel U.S. Route 2, the "High Line." Eight miles east of Minot, a small city much maligned in North Dakota weather jokes, the *Empire Builder* passes the Surrey cutoff, where the line coming from Grand Forks and Devils Lake joins the proper main from New Rockford, a faster and shorter route used by the *Empire Builder* before Amtrak. From here west it is a single line to Seattle.

Except to Hill, its builder, and the Burlington Northern, its present owner, the line is a little-appreciated piece of railroad, through a little-appreciated part of America. Of all the trans-Mississippi Wests, this northern tier of North Dakota and Montana suffers most from an "out back" image, and to most rail travelers not from this region the experience of riding across it confirms prejudices about western remoteness and endlessly boring open space. The perception is partly an unfortunate result of scheduling: because at this latitude the Rocky Mountains lie several hundred miles farther west than they do to the south, the *Empire Builder*, running on much the same timetable as the *California Zephyr* from Chicago to Denver and Salt Lake City, traverses in both directions this high-plains landscape entirely in daylight. For easterners looking for the thrills of mountain scenery, this route always disappoints, as derisory comments in the lounge car about "this dreary trip" attest. Other parts of the West resemble it, but the rail traveler is seldom afforded such an extended view of them. The reaction reflects an unfortunate geographical and historical ignorance about the West, whose vastness is its point. To watch it drift past a train window at fifty to sixty miles per hour, from sunrise to sunset, is to touch this vastness. That few see what they are looking at, while sad for them, has, however, the positive result of keeping this a country where few linger long. So it has stayed unspoiled, known chiefly to those who live there, who in most cases have lived there for a long time.

West from Minot their presence is marked by far-scattered farmsteads, arrow-straight highways, an occasional farm implement amid a vast expanse of plowed black earth or waving wheat. At Stanley the *Empire Builder* observes its scheduled stop with a ten-second pause; at Tioga (no longer even a flag stop) flares burn excess gas from the wells in the Williston Basin. Williston itself is a fair-sized town, a railroad division point and, during the early 1950s and then again in the early 1970s, a small version of Calgary or Houston: a boomtown built on oil. Today the boom has ended, as vacant motels and fast-food eateries along over-built highway strips mutely witness. But down at the red-brick depot at the foot of Main Street, little changes. In the tidy station park, tall trees shade an old Mikado-type locomotive, a gift to Williston from the Great Northern in 1958, the very end of the steam era, and a World War I memorial inscribed to "the Boys of Williams County" with plaques added for other wars through the 1960s. Williston once saw two daily passenger trains each way; now there is just one. But here you can still step aboard a Pullman bound for Glacier Park or Seattle, the Twin Cities or Chicago.

Leaving Williston at midmorning, the westbound *Empire Builder* begins its day-long run across northern Montana. For the attentive traveler it is a treasure. Between Williston and the Continental Divide at the other end of Montana stretch nearly five hundred miles of high plains — a flat to gently rolling vastness in shades of brown, green, and gold. Montana's skies are legend and like everything else about this state very large. And there was no better vantage on them than the dome cars of the 1950s *Empire Builder*. Although today's train is poorer in this as in most other amenities, its Pullmans offer a smoothly swaying ride that is like nothing so much as being at sea. Landfall is the mountains, far distant; en route is a voyage across, in Willa Cather's words, "the floor of the sky." Small stations, most of which saw their last passenger years go, dot the line every ten miles or so, reciting in their names the record of settlement and in some cases abandonment as well: Bainville, Brockton, Poplar, Oswego, Savoy, Kremlin, Rudyard, Inverness, Devon, Dunkirk. Where the train still does stop, rituals as old as the West are still kept. At Wolf Point (where a short platform necessitates two stops: one for the coaches and one for the Pullmans), three Indians lounge beside a grain elevator; one of them peddles a drawing (of an Indian) to the sleeping-car porter (a Hispanic), who remarks to his white passengers that the Indian will no doubt just go out and buy fire-water with his earnings. Small "restored" herds of buffalo appear from time to time; highway signs warn of "Cattle at Large"; antelope roam. At Glasgow, beyond the white and green brick station lies the Mint Bar (Montana's nickname is the Treasure State, for its mineral

The only animal ever to adorn a railroad logo in America, the Great Northern's "Rocky" the rocky mountain goat graced everything from boxcars to tickets and playing cards until the Great Northern's merger with the Burlington Northern in 1970.

wealth). At Malta, where painter Charles Russell once rendered many a western scene, the scene on this particular day presented visiting circus elephants, an old Carnegie Library, and the Maltana Hotel. Havre (pronounced Haver), another division point, comes in midafternoon and still has the feel of an old-fashioned station stop: enough time for a stroll down a fine Montana main street while crews service the train.

From Havre the grade rises gently but noticeably as the Rockies draw near. At Shelby you are at 3,283 feet and climbing; at Cut Bank, in the foothills, at 3,753; at the summit, sixty miles away, at 5,213. In between, old station names like Gunsight, Sundance, Meriwether (after Lewis), Blackfoot (after the Indians), Triple Divide (after the peak whose runoff divides among the Atlantic, Pacific, and Arctic oceans), Bison, and Rising Wolf resound with the history of the region. A monument to Hill's engineer John F. Stevens and to Teddy Roosevelt adorns the summit, and as the *Empire Builder* winds its way down the west side of Marias Pass along the Flathead river, you peer (on the right going west) into the vast wilderness of Glacier National Park.

Among the West's scenic wonders that the transcontinental railroads deliberately associated with their trains, those that the Great Northern could lay claim to were not of the first order. With proprietary instincts, the Santa Fe staked out the Grand Canyon; the Union Pacific the wonders of Bryce and Zion; the Denver & Rio Grande Western the Colorado Rockies; the Northern Pacific the geysers and grizzlies of Yellowstone. Jim Hill's line offered only Glacier, aptly named for its sixty or so living glaciers, but whose scenery, while lovely, does not dazzle in quite the same way as do the mountains farther south. What the Great Northern did manage to say for years, quite correctly and quite exclusively, was that it was the only transcontinental route whose mainline edged a national park: Glacier. The Great Northern skirts the park's southern boundary for some sixty miles, and during the park season of mid-June to mid-September at least one of its passenger trains has always stopped at both eastern and western entrances.

Both gateways vividly conjure up another age of travel. From the log station at East Glacier, where befeathered Blackfeet off the neighboring reservation once met alighting tourists, it was but a short walk past gardens of larkspur and columbine to Glacier Park Lodge, an immense timber hotel dating from early in the century. From the West Glacier stop at Belton, it was but a short ride into the park and the lodge at Lake MacDonald, a smaller hostelry originally built as a hunting lodge and strewn with the stuffed and mounted elk, bear, mountain sheep, and goats to prove it. (The mountain goat also occupied a place of great corporate distinction, at the center of the Great Northern's logo from the earliest days until the Great Northern ceased to be a separate entity in 1970. "Rocky," as he was known, was the only animal ever so honored by an American railroad.) Such places belong to the railway age, a fact most evident here in Glacier where the trains are still close at hand.

Today's *Empire Builder* makes these seasonal stops, and Amtrak promotes the park for the same reasons the Great Northern once did. The "fit," in a sense, is more perfect than ever, since both Amtrak and the national parks are today very democratic operations. In this the era of the camper, the recreational vehicle or RV, and the summer family vacation as the habit of people of all classes and tastes, the parks have followed and have become like their market. Our modern taste no longer demands such resplendent buildings as these great lodges. They were conceived as adornments to wilderness when wilderness was still a romantic adornment to civilization, and not merely part of "the environment."

One place remains, however, that manages to finesse the cultural distance between the years of its origin and its current status. It works better because of the railroad, which, here, still links past and present. Down the western side of Marias Pass, eighteen miles from the summit, lies Essex. Since the building of the Great Northern, Essex has been a "helper station," where helper locomotives were kept to push heavy trains to the summit. It was a ritual of mountain railroading — extra engines boosting big trains over the top — common in the age of steam, but here at Essex it has survived in much of its glory into the high-horsepower diesel era. Steam railroading was labor-intensive in the extreme, especially in mountains in winter. Along this section of the Great Northern's mainline yearly snowfall averaged some 240 inches in the 1930s, and the railroaders required to man and direct the big plows and locomotives stationed at Essex then included engine crews, roadmasters, trainmasters, building engineers, mechanics, and carpenters. The Izaak Walton Inn, built by a Great Northern subsidiary in 1939 to accommodate them, stands today as their monument. Happily, it still functions, housing the smaller crews of the big green Burlington Northern diesels that idle in the yards in front of the inn, and welcoming travelers ready for a quiet,

In the 1930s porters from the Glacier Park Hotel and befeathered Indians welcomed tourists who wished to see the wilderness but with all the civilized touches.

In northwestern Montana, where the Great Plains meet the Rocky Mountains, the Great Northern Railway built Glacier Park Hotel, a timbered monument to the time when to travel meant to go by train. Teepees from the nearby Blackfoot reservation adorn the lawns, viewed early in the century from Glacier Park Station, where passengers still alight.

unpretentious refuge amid a million acres of wilderness. A solid log half-timber structure of thirty-some rooms, the Izaak Walton was also built in anticipation of the opening of a third, middle entrance to Glacier National Park, something forgotten with the onset of World War II and never again revived. Yet the inn survives and, thanks to the successful campaign of the current innkeepers to have Essex made a flag stop for the *Empire Builder*, it is now possible to travel there conveniently by train. Given the history of the place, it is the only way to arrive. Sadly the old white Essex depot no longer serves passengers, reportedly because the fact that the public has to cross the tracks to get to the inn raised questions of liability. But the innkeeper meets you at a new halt a quarter-mile up the line; he offers honest food and lodging at a fair price; and the view from his front porch, if you have a fancy for trains and sweet mountain air, is incomparable.

That was how the Great Northern described the *Empire Builder* of the 1950s: incomparable. And there are still aging fomer Great Northern crewmen around who feel it was a big mistake to have replaced it all so early. They believe that, properly refurbished, those trains had a lot of miles left in them yet. Surely they did, and they succumbed more to the mandate of standardization in the now nationalized passenger system and the economies that go with it than to age itself. But as long as at least the name endures, then something of history's richness will, too.

A little more history of this northern transcontinental reveals two other train names, today long vanished from the timetable, whose shades are fitting to contemplate here at the crest of the Rockies, the divide between East and West. In the 1950s and 1960s the Great Northern ran a second streamliner daily from St. Paul to Seattle. It was a comfortable maid-of-all-work that did a lot of mail and express business and whose summertime consist swelled with tourists bound for the park. A western train, it shared a name (accidentally for sure) with a poem by Stephen Vincent Benet, "Western Star."

Another old Great Northern limited carried a name redolent of another kind of western connection. The *Oriental Limited*, in the 1910s and 1920s the Great Northern's premier train, symbolized associations that old Jim Hill hoped were another justification for building the Great Northern in the first place, associations that persist today, a century later, in phrases like "Pacific Rim." Hill had seen Seattle as a gateway to Japan and the Far East, and for a time even operated a fleet of transpacific steamships meant to extend the reach of his western railroad beyond the West to the East. The notion was exotic, pioneering, and, like everything Hill did, undertaken with great cunning and confidence. The *Oriental Limited* for a time featured kimono-clad Japanese hostesses serving tea in the lounge. But for Hill's great silk trains with their perishable cargo of raw Japanese silk bound for clothiers in the American East, even the *Oriental Limited* took the siding.

Though raw silk is no longer transported by rail, Hill's perception about the East was correct and prescient. For as today's *Empire Builder* descends the western slope of the Rockies, crosses Spokane's Inland Empire, crests the Cascades and descends sharply from the Cascade Tunnel through misty evergreen forests to sea level, it is plain that this world is as remote from the American East as it was in Hill's time. Partly it is distance, which is still great (1,782 miles back to St. Paul), partly it is climate, and partly it is spirit. The *Empire Builder* reaches salt water at Everett, Washington, an old milltown thirty-three miles north of Seattle, where a Japanese ship, the *Fugi Angel*, loads timber. Out in Puget Sound the stately old *Princess Marguerite*, built in Scotland for the Canadian Pacific in the 1940s, still

Wicker met electric lights in the observation car of the *North Coast Limited*. Inaugurated in 1900, it ran between Chicago and Seattle every day for the next seventy-one years.

plies north to Victoria, British Columbia; yacht basins dot the shoreline; the forest comes down to meet the sea. A place on the sea (and the closest American port to both Alaska and the Orient), Seattle looks outward across it; in this case, westward toward the East. Once a provincial town filled with Scandinavian migrants from the Dakotas and Montana, Seattle today is a Pacific city, with the oriental faces and a casual, laid-back air of post-sixties California to prove it. Ecology-conscious, ethnically diverse, and democratic, it is not the place Hill knew, or would particularly have liked. But it is still the terminus for the train that bears his sobriquet — still endpoint for the last of the transcontinental railroads.

If Seattle now looks out to the Pacific more keenly than it does back to the prairies and the cities of the East, it is only reflecting the larger shift in our common attention from the things of this continent to the things of another one. For Hill and men of his age and ilk, the Orient was a market, a place to trade, and for some an object to convert. In an era that worships cultural pluralism, conversion is a bit out of fashion, but the fundamental fact of trade is little changed whatever its shifting balances. The Orient has become, or is now perceived to be, along with the whole American West Coast, part of the Pacific Rim, a newly invented geographical entity with only water at its center and a polyglot of countries or parts of countries at its edges. A sort of continent without a heart, it is a fitting abstraction for an age that abhors any hint of ethnocentrism, and to which distance as an obstacle has little meaning. On this new continent (over which Amtrak offers some nice views between Everett and San Diego) there will obviously be no railroads. Therefore, the transcontinental railroads represent the ultimate abridgement of distance. Jets and rockets abridge greater distances, to be sure, at greater speeds, but they have not the slightest connection with what it is they abridge, with what is "in between." More than any other of the transcontinentals, Hill's Great Northern sprang from the "in between" and was sustained by it: the great open spaces where he built his empire.

A distance of some fourteen hundred miles separates the most northerly of the transcontinentals, the Great Northern, from the most southerly, the Southern Pacific's Sunset route. They share a low esteem by many travelers, but otherwise are vastly different. Consider the endpoints. The *Empire Builder* commences in Chicago in the classic cave

of the greatest of the union stations (built in 1925 and still bustling with trains), close by the Chicago River, a stream more dignified by its bascule bridges than anything else. The *Sunset Limited* begins in New Orleans in the muraled openness of a station built in 1952, now dubbed the Transportation Center and shared with buses, close by the Mississippi River, a stream whose dignity changes little with time. The *Empire Builder* ends in Seattle, clean cool capital of the Pacific Northwest, at the degraded King Street Station in the shadow of a sports dome. The *Sunset* ties up in Los Angeles Union Passenger Terminal, that still-handsome prop from the heyday of Hollywood and the railroads (1939), close to streets where mostly Spanish will be heard and to a snazzy new Japanese hotel. So with the in between. The *Empire Builder* traverses high plains and green northern mountains; the *Sunset* passes through coastal swamps, Texas badlands, and southwestern deserts.

All the western trains are now Amtrak-issue Superliners (a lame effort at stylishness in naming if ever there was one, and infinitely inferior to the older "streamliner," which became generic for all first-class trains of the 1940s and 1950s). Compared with the custom-built domes, diners, and Pullmans of thirty years ago, Amtrak's Superliner-

The full-length dome cars introduced for Pullman passengers on the Great Northern's *Empire Builder* in 1955 were the apex of postwar streamlined luxury and a measure of how hard the railroads tried to keep the passenger business. The cars seated seventy-five on angled sofa seats upstairs and had a cocktail lounge below.

equipped *Empire Builder*, in which there is no china in the diner and no glassware in the club car, is a spartan affair. The *Sunset* offers nothing better and suffers the added indignity of operating only three days a week. So it was with special pleasure that I made this journey aboard a private car, a fine luxury in these days of diminished comforts and the only way remaining to experience train travel untouched by the tastes and economies of the 1980s. This particular car was built by Pullman in 1926 as a business car for the Santa Fe; it rolled on six-wheel trucks, and weighed a hundred tons. Configured to provide space and comfort for a few, it contained a galley and a butler's pantry, crew quarters for cook and steward, a dining room seating eight, staterooms sleeping five, a solarium lounge, and an open platform. There are some two hundred such private cars operating in America; their owners have their own organization, the American Association of Private Railroad Car Owners, Inc., which publishes its own bimonthly magazine, *Private Varnish*, and holds an annual convention. In recent years these meetings have attracted at least a score of private cars, ranging from sleek dome-observations built for the old *California Zephyr*, to heavy-weight wood-paneled majesties like "Chapel Hill," built for Marjorie Post in the 1920s. Some are the toys of rich men; others belong to syndicates that work them in the charter trade. To Amtrak, which charges a hefty mileage fee to pull them on one of its trains, they mean several million dollars of revenue a year. So privilege serves the people.

The private cars represent dreams and prompt visions of other times, not unlike, in some respects, the journey across this oldest, southernmost part of the West. It was across this West — what would become Texas, New Mexico, and Arizona — that white men first wandered, looking for cities of gold in the sixteenth century. It was along the valley of the Rio Grande that Spanish fathers made Catholics of red men in the seventeenth and eighteenth. It was verdant east Texas that was such a magnet for southern expansionism in the days of the Cotton Kingdom in the first half of the nineteenth. Properly speaking, during the Spanish era this was not West at all, but North, the metropolitan centers of power lying far to the south in Mexico and beyond. But with American independence and the national growth that followed, the perspective shifted, and Texas beckoned to the ambitious and discontented from faraway Kentucky, Tennessee, Alabama, and Mississippi. Fame followed at the Alamo in San Antonio in 1836, and Texas became first an independent nation, then a spoil of the Mexican War in the 1840s, and finally another of a growing number of western states — but, of course, the biggest. Both southern and western, Texas left the Union to fight for the Confederacy in the Civil War, which returns us to the subject of the railroad.

It was the drive for western expansion and the debate over which kind of America — the modernist free-state North or the traditionalist slave-holding South — should be reproduced there that explains the early railroad history of this West. As the controversy between North and South heated up in the 1850s, each section saw a transcontinental railroad as a tool for shaping the West in its own image and for bringing the new states there into its own web of economic and political interest. There was, of course, no railroad until after the Civil War, and then it commenced in Council Bluffs, Iowa, in the center of the country, with direct ties to Yankee Chicago. But Southerners had hoped, not unreasonably, to begin things in New Orleans, run west through Texas, then across the Gadsden Purchase (acquired from Mexico in 1854 just so a railroad could be built there), to finally meet the Pacific at San Diego or Los Angeles. The United States War Department, then headed by Jefferson Davis, the future president of the Confederacy, surveyed the route in detail, but the time was not yet right. When it was, twenty years later, the dream of southern independence was as dead as slavery, and the route never again had about it the same aura of vital necessity.

New Orleans, then and now, does not look naturally to the west, but rather lies on a transportation axis reaching northward up the Mississippi Valley by rail or water to Memphis and St. Louis, and southward and southeastward out across the Gulf of Mexico to Latin America and Europe. Back in the days when cotton was king and English mills were its market, New Orleans became a major port, even though a hundred miles upriver from the Gulf itself. Later it was headquarters of the United Fruit Company, reputed owner of much of Central America and of the banana boats that unloaded their cargoes along its wharves. In our own time a parade of ships flying many flags glides past its levee to the refineries and chemical complexes that dot the shoreline all the way to Baton Rouge.

The fact that it is a coastal city means that the rail line connecting it with Los Angeles is, as a glance at the map will show, a truly transcontinental line: coast to coast and ocean to ocean. (The other three "transcontinental" passenger routes have for their eastern terminus Chicago, at the heart

The most storied of the western railroads, the Santa Fe never served its namesake town in New Mexico, but it did trade on the historical association of the Old Santa Fe Trail, which its rails crossed in Burlingame, Kansas.

of the continent, not its edge, and 800 miles from tidewater.) Los Angeles, 2,033 miles west from New Orleans, looks out on a vastly different world: not the old Europe of Frenchmen, Italians, Germans, Spaniards, and Jews, but the Pacific world of Japanese, Chinese, Filipinos, Koreans, and, closer at hand, Mexicans. Whichever end of the line, ethnic diversity doesn't get much richer.

In between, however, it is nature's hand, not man's, that commands most respect and holds the traveler's eye: the mighty Mississippi making its crescent bend at New Orleans as viewed from the Huey P. Long Bridge; Louisiana swamps where alligators sun themselves on hot railroad ballast; Texas vastness fit for the widest screen (the film version of Edna Ferber's *Giant* was shot at a west Texas site near the route of the *Sunset*, with Rock Hudson bringing Elizabeth Taylor, his new Virginia bride, home to Texas in a private car); the muddy Rio Grande, a stream as far as possible in fact and spirit from the Mississippi; the desert serenity of southern New Mexico and Arizona at night. Along the way lie some remarkable towns, too: New Iberia, Louisiana, home of Tabasco Sauce; Houston, whose fortunes rise and fall with the price of crude; San Antonio of Alamo fame and with a mission-style station to match; El Paso, "that west Texas town," as the song says; Lordsburg, New Mexico, where the Hidalgo Hotel offers "cleanliness for less"; Tucson, where the Arizona Inn still caters to the carriage trade of the 1920s; Phoenix, where the new Arizona, watered by the Colorado River, proved itself; Yuma, where you cross that Colorado River and enter California.

California is it — the end of the dream, as they say, and the end of the line. Two other transcontinental passenger lines also end here, one in Los Angeles, the other in San Francisco. From Los Angeles to Chicago you can ride all the way on the rails of the Atchison, Topeka & Santa Fe, the only passenger route from Chicago that doesn't involve two or more different railroads. East through the Cajon Pass, Flagstaff, Albuquerque, Raton Pass, and Kansas City, this was once the route of the lordly *Super Chief*, which at its zenith in the 1940s and 1950s shared renown only with the New York Central's *Twentieth Century Limited* as the finest train in America. Until the late fifties, it was all-Pullman and extra-fare — and fast (thirty-nine hours). Movie stars and moguls made the *Super Chief* famous; the Santa Fe management back in Chicago made it work and was proud of it. Indeed, defense of its reputation (or the memory of its reputation) occasioned one of the last demonstrations of real moxie by an American railroad on behalf of passenger service. So much of the Santa Fe's corporate image and public good will were tied to the famous train that the Santa Fe tied conditioned use by Amtrak of the name *Super Chief* on the maintenance of a certain level of service. When Amtrak removed the first-class diner to save money, the Santa Fe, much to its credit, called in the first-class name. Running for a few years with the colorless name *Southwest Limited*, it now is known as the *Southwest Chief*, a slight improvement but a pale imitation of former grandeur.

It is, however, still relatively fast. Speed in fact once undid it, when in October 1979 an inattentive engineer unfamiliar with a new routing sent the *Southwest Limited*, née *Super Chief*, careening into a thirty-mile-per-hour curve at close to eighty, spilling much of the train across the backyards of Lawrence, Kansas. Two crew members were killed; my wife and I, both passengers, survived. A major, though not the largest, accident in Amtrak's history, it points out for one who attended it much that recommends the safety of rail travel. A high-speed wreck that puts twelve of seventeen cars "on the ground," in railroad parlance, is a serious wreck. Much damage is done: track curls like hairpins; ballast plows up; adjacent buildings are plowed into; the acrid smell of brakeshoe smoke fills the air. Yet most people walk away only slightly injured, if mightily wrought-up.

Two key facts distinguish rail transport from its competition, airplanes and automobiles. First, in an accident, there is no fire, which in plane crashes virtually assures death to anyone surviving impact. Second, trains have great structural strength, which is hardly a strong suit among automobile manufacturers, as those gruesome anti–drunk driving ads testify. If you take a seventy-ton stainless steel Pullman car and tip it off the track at eighty miles per hour, chances are you can fairly promptly pick it up, set it on temporary trucks, and roll it off to the shop to have the dents hammered out and the windows replaced. The injuries sustained in such a vehicle are those of concussion: consider the dynamic of the ballbearing bouncing around in the tin can. The bumps and bruises hurt a lot, but seldom kill or even wound seriously. Little crushes or collapses; victims may have to be hoisted out on backboards, but few have to be pried loose or cut free.

Such major accidents as Amtrak has suffered can usually be ascribed to excessive speed, bad track, or unprotected crossings. Yet trains are terribly safe, and have been ever since the introduction decades ago of the air brake, the

The last of the transcontinental lines, the Great Northern pushed through Washington's Cascade Mountain in 1892.

Chinese laborers shovel snow for Northern Pacific tracklaying crews near the summit of the Cascade range in 1886. The railroads often hired affordable and available Chinese workers to build the western lines.

automatic block signal, and the steel passenger car. The chances that an Amtrak passenger will be involved in an accident, and that if so he or she will be seriously hurt or killed, are so extremely remote that safety might well be one of Amtrak's chief selling points. So it was long ago with the Pullman Company: "Travel and Sleep in Safety and Comfort" went the company slogan, emblazoned on hat bags and matchbooks. Sadly, both then and now, safety was not enough to counter, in the judgment of most travelers, the convenience of the automobile or the speed of the airplane. Passenger train wrecks do, however, make good press stories: they are more exotic than either plane or car crashes. Some horrifying pile of upended passenger cars has much the same visual impact as a sharply listing ocean liner bound for the bottom (something the world last saw in 1956 when the *Andrea Dorea* went down). What is seldom remarked about, with trains or ships, is the amazing fact that most people walk away, physically little the worse for wear.

Until the coming of the transcontinental railroads, that was just how most people crossed the plains and mountains en route to their various promised lands: they walked at the plodding pace of the oxen or mules or horses that pulled their wagons over rutted tracks in prairie grass. Railroads later upped the speed of land transportation by a factor of five to ten times. From time immemorial, people had moved at five miles per hour; on the trains they rode at twenty-five to fifty. There would not again be so great a leap until the introduction of the commercial jet in our own day. The jet sealed the fate of the unsubsidized passenger train as decisively as the railroad had assured the demise of the stagecoach and the Pony Express. The space of exactly a century separated these two analogous developments, which gives to this consideration of railroads in America a special historical resonance. Today Amtrak's four transcontinental passenger trains are the remnants of something no longer palpable in our imagination or economy. As "modern" as they may be, they are, in fact, artifacts: a vital cultural resource utterly irrelevant to the commerce of the country. To ride them at fifty miles per hour across two thousand miles of vast plains, mountains, and deserts that are routinely flown over at five hundred miles per hour is to experience a certain remoteness from current history, which itself seems to move faster now in all respects than in the railway age. By contrast, to have ridden a transcontinental train in 1869, the year the first line was completed, must have been to sense what it was like to be at the very crest of history — the place where it was really happening and likely to happen for a long time to come.

Thus, here, the first of the transcontinentals comes last. Its story (the Union Pacific/Central Pacific route between Omaha and Sacramento) is the most often told and most clichéd of all railroad sagas. Most of the original route is no longer accessible to today's rail traveler: only between Salt Lake City and Oakland does Amtrak's *California Zephyr* approximate the historical route of the first transcontinental. The Chicago & North Western from Chicago to Omaha, the original connecting line from the Missouri River to the East, is freight-only, and so with the Union Pacific's line west from Omaha to North Platte, Cheyenne, and across Wyoming to Utah's Great Basin. The *California Zephyr* today is Amtrak's most popular train because of its famous all-daylight run through the Colorado Rockies between Denver and Salt Lake. But the line as first imagined and built had less to do with scenery than with three urgent concerns of that time: the need to tie the new and rich state of California to the Union as the Civil War approached; the lure of Asiatic commerce that would make the United States the land bridge for trade between Europe and the Orient; and the drive for Manifest Destiny, that peculiarly American version of a nineteenth-century impulse that had to do with subduing Kipling's lesser breeds and extending a benign Western dominion to all manner of remote places. Manifest Destiny was as accepted a notion then as cultural pluralism is today. As a measure of their difference, only Manifest Destiny could have accounted for so prodigious a feat as the building of the transcontinental. Cultural pluralism surely would have prevented its construction, dooming, as it did for all time, the Indians.

Financed with benefit of elaborate federal subsidy and private financial sleight of hand, the line advanced from both ends, Sacramento and Council Bluffs, Iowa, toward a meeting point somewhere in between. From the time Abraham Lincoln signed the Pacific Railway Act on July 1, 1862, it was nearly seven years till the famous gold spike at last joined the Central Pacific and the Union Pacific at Promontory Summit in Utah. Since little work was possible while the Civil War raged, construction was actually completed in less than four years. Seventeen hundred seventy-six miles of track built with human and animal power through hostile wilderness: epic achievement of a high order. It excited the

The Dale Creek Bridge in 1868. Built on the Union Pacific's mainline in Wyoming with precut timber from Michigan, the bridge was 126 feet above the streambed and had to be guyed with ropes and wires.

Citadel Rock and bridge over Green River. Construction of the Union Pacific across the high plains of Wyoming in the late 1860s put existing railroad technology to the test. Of all nature's obstacles, distance was the greatest.

imagination of the nation, this peacetime army of engineers, surveyors, graders, and tracklayers — northerners, southerners, Irish, and Chinese — forging the rails across the continent. Subsidies were tied to mileage of track laid, and the incentives were considerable for speedy if not quality construction.

While the intent was for the two companies to build to where they met, that point was not named in the law, and by the time it was decided that the actual joining of the rails would be at Promontory Summit, northwest of Ogden, competing crews had actually finished some 225 miles of parallel grades, moving past each other in opposite directions. As the two lines approached the designated site on April 28, 1869, a Central Pacific crew, drilled as if it were a military company, succeeded in laying ten miles and fifty-six feet of track in a single day, a record for the enterprise. The final meeting of the East and West took place at a carefully orchestrated ceremony May 10, 1869, a moment caught by the photographer then, and recreated by Cecil B. deMille seventy years later in his epic *Union Pacific*. The image is famous: the Union Pacific's American-style locomotive #119 nudging up to the Central Pacific's diamond-stack *Jupiter*; chief engineers Samuel S. Montague of the Central Pacific and Grenville M. Dodge of the Union Pacific shaking hands; champagne bottles extended. A tie of polished California laurel was predrilled to receive four ceremonial spikes: two gold from California; a silver from Nevada; an alloy of gold, silver, and iron from Arizona. But it was the last, plain iron spike in an ordinary tie that triggered the telegrapher's simple message: "Done."

The line through Promontory served as the mainline of the Southern Pacific (which had absorbed the Central Pacific) for thirty-five years, until completion of the Lucin cutoff in 1904, which carried the rails across the middle of Great Salt Lake. The old line was used when bad weather threatened the cutoff and survived until 1942, when its rails were pulled up to make tanks and Liberty Ships for the war effort. Were it still available, the line might have found use yet, as record-high lake levels have threatened the Lucin Line. Promontory Summit itself is today a designated national historic site, with a small museum and a short section of track where in summer replicas of #119 and *Jupiter* reenact the completion of the first transcontinental. The closest Amtrak comes is Ogden. Now, as then, it is a remarkably desolate spot: in winter, it is vacant of visitors, the trains and tracks long gone, only the grades and cuts dating from spring 1869 still visible. But of all the places associated with railroads in America, Promontory more than any other cries out, in silence, that without a doubt something really happened here.

You reach it by car west from Brigham City, Utah, on State Route 83, which also leads to the Utah test site of the Morton Thiokol Company, makers of rocket engines for the space shuttle. The signs to each are adjacent and are caught in the eye or the camera's lens in a single glance. Depending on your biases, it is either a thrilling or depressing coincidence, this dramatic butting up of late-nineteenth-against late-twentieth-century technology in the Promontory Mountains. It probably heightens the impact of what you see at the Gold Spike site itself, abandoned as it is, a reminder of how the world moved on decisively to other enthusiasms. It also reminds one of the exploratory nature of these transcontinental railroads, which bridged the last American wilderness, helped build the cities, break the sod, create the wealth. This was exploration based on the gambler's hunch that the cards were indeed there, that there really was something out there, different, for sure, from what men already knew about and possessed, but which could be made their own. It proved a sound hunch then. Now, who knows?

Amtrak's stainless steel *Empire Builder* slices through the vast wheat fields of North Dakota.

Preceding pages: The wealth of the
Great Plains is wheat; the grain
elevator its ubiquitous symbol. The
functional patterns of wheat farming in Crosby, North Dakota, are
relieved by a veteran of a demoli-
tion derby.

The journey on the top deck of
Amtrak's superliners over the vast
spaces of the West is akin to a sea
voyage. In Williston, North Dakota
a western family embarks on the
Empire Builder for such a trip.

Typical of recycled stations, the
Rock Island depot in Lincoln,
Nebraska, once serviced by the
Rock Island *Rockets*, is now home
to a local bank.

Boyhood and trains go together.
A young North Dakota farm lad
watches, much as his grandparents
did, as a local freight carries out the
wheat.

In North Dakota, a western sky and light render a workaday branch-line locomotive into something theatrical.

In the mural, partially visible text reads:

WEST-BOUND
DEPICTS THE DENVER ZEPHYR,
A TRAIN THAT INCLUDED CRESTON IN
THE REGULAR CHICAGO TO DENVER ROUTE
DURING THE 30'S AND 40'S.
THE BRIDGE KNOWN AS THE ARMITAGE
OR PARTY BRIDGE BY THE LOCAL YOUTH,
IS LOCATED 1 MILE WEST OF TOWN.
THE COOP GRAIN ELEVATOR,
A SYMBOL OF THE AREA
FARMING INDUSTRY,
WAS 'MOVED' INTO VIEW
AND IS ACTUALLY FURTHER
TO THE RIGHT.

The Artist:
Juli Johnson
8/81

A SPECIAL THANKS TO FAMILY
AND FRIENDS, WHO GENEROUSLY
DONATED TIME AND
MATERIALS.

In Creston, Iowa, on the route of today's *California Zephyr*, a local mural memorializes the famous *Burlington Zephyr*. The world's first diesel-electric streamlined train in 1934 traveled the 1,015 miles from Denver, Colorado, to Chicago non-stop at an average speed of 77.6 mph. (The train is now preserved at the Museum of Science and Industry in Chicago.)

Weather and graffiti give a patina to bridgework near Skykomish, Washington, on the Great Northern. Bridges have long been backdrops for commercial art and more recently, since the advent of the spray can, common graffiti.

Following pages: Heavy long grades and trains still necessitate helper engines to move freights over mountain passes. Here a Burlington Northern helper unit returns to Essex, Montana, from Marias Pass; trestle and trusswork bridge the Flathead River.

Mainline switches are kept clear of
snow by gas or electricity; on the
sidings the job is still done by a
worker with a broom.

In winter a ballast-spreader can become a snowplow. Such equipment is required where annual snowfall can reach 200 inches. The Burlington Northern's mainline follows the southern boundary of Glacier National Park, which still boasts fifty "living glaciers."

Opposite: Two small towns along the route of the *Empire Builder*: Rugby, North Dakota *(above)*, a typical farming community but also the geographical center of North America and, 1,239 miles to the west, Skykomish, Washington *(below)*, where until 1956 electric locomotives took trains right through the Cascade Tunnel, which at 7.79 miles is the longest in North America.

Above: Transcontinental railroading requires engineering feats even today. When a massive landslide blocked the Denver & Rio Grande Western's mainline near Thistle, Utah, for three months in 1983, a six-mile bypass was constructed, including new tunnels through Billy's Mountain.

One of the branch lines that built
Jim Hill's empire, Great Northern
tracks reach west to Crosby, North
Dakota.

The *Empire Builder* enters Montana along the Missouri River near its junction with the Yellowstone. Explorers Meriwether Lewis and William Clark and countless Indians before them passed this way. Train travelers today will be in Montana—the third-largest state in the union and famed for its mines and ranches—for nearly twelve hours and 700 miles.

Left: A General Motors–Electric-Motive Division "Geep" or general purpose freight locomotive, a type common to almost every railroad in America: a no-frills approach to industrial design.

Above: Freight coupling gear.

IT'S UP
TO YOU

CAPY

L.D.LM

LT. WT

Before the opening of the Moffat Tunnel in 1927, trains used to labor their way up the "Giant's Ladder" to 11,680-foot Rollins Pass in the Colorado Rockies (*above*), the highest point ever reached by a standard-gauge railroad in North America. Named for Colorado railroad builder David Moffat, who died years before, the tunnel, at an elevation of 9,239 feet, is still the highest crossing of the Continental Divide by any of the western railroads. At 6.2 miles, it is the third-longest bore in North America after the Cascade and Flathead tunnels in Montana.

Preceding pages: A Rio Grande freight emerges from the east portal. Curving sharply right to the north is the track of the old line to Rollins Pass, still accessible by dirt road.

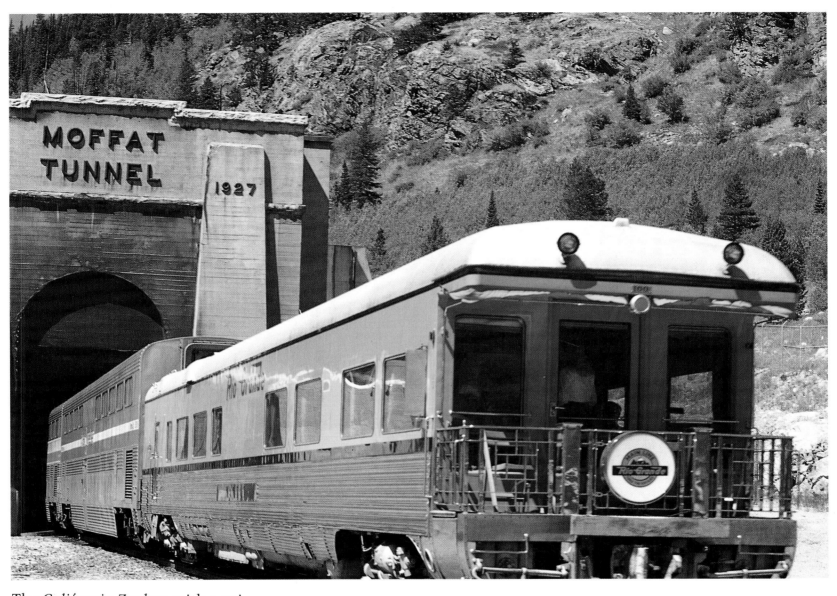

The *California Zephyr*, with a private car in tow, enters the Moffat Tunnel, fifty miles west from and some 4,000 feet above Denver.

Left: Created and sustained by the Denver & Rio Grande Western, the town of Helper, Utah, is a division point and home for helper engines that boost heavy freights up over 7,440-foot Soldier Summit, the top of the Wasatch range.

Above: The Humboldt River, seen here near Carlin, Nevada, rises in the mountains of northern Nevada, but its waters never reach the sea. The tracks of the Union Pacific and Southern Pacific railroads parallel much of its winding course through a wild landscape before it disappears in the Humboldt sink.

Freight steam engines were almost always black, but since the diesel era, locomotives have carried the distinctive color schemes and graphics of their owning roads. Here the Santa Fe's latest colors appear on a twelve-wheel high-horsepower locomotive.

Semaphore signals (the vertical arm
means all clear; diagonal, caution;
horizontal, stop) have been widely
displaced by simpler lights. They
linger, however, on some western
roads, as on the Santa Fe near
Wagon Mound, New Mexico, where
the train passes through lonely and
legendary ranch country and along
remnants of the old Santa Fe Trail.

Elaborate snow fencing on the Union Pacific's line is required to hold back the heavy snow drifts common in this windswept high country. Huts shelter maintenance crews and equipment at Dale, Wyoming.

Sherman Hill in Wyoming, one of the most famous railroad grades in the world, was once home territory of the world's largest steam locomotives: the "Big Boys" built by the American Locomotive Company for the Union Pacific in the early 1940s (130 feet in length and weighing 1,120,000 pounds). Later, Sherman Hill also saw the world's longest

(96 feet) and most powerful (6,600 horsepower) single-unit diesel-electric locomotive: the Union Pacific's "Centennial" type introduced in 1969, the hundredth anniversary of the completion of the first transcontinental railroad. This line through the high mountain plateaus of southern Wyoming is today regrettably "freight only."

Following pages: A steam crane and tenders in Ogden, Utah, proclaim the riveted ruggedness and sheer massiveness of railroading in the West.

Initials marked with stones or painted on rock commonly identify small western towns. In Nevada, Elko (note the white "E" on the hill) takes its name from an Indian word meaning "white woman." A Southern Pacific train heads east loaded with lumber. The *California Zephyr* also passes here, but at night.

The ubiquitous steel truss bridge is an icon of the railroad across every landscape in America. Newly painted with aluminum, this one stands in the Humboldt Valley.

Climbing east over Utah's Wasatch
Mountains through a series of horseshoe curves to Soldier Summit
(7,440 feet), the *California Zephyr*
begins a day-long journey to Denver
through some of the most spectacular mountain scenery in America.

Climbing west from Denver, the
California Zephyr begins its fifty-
mile ascent up the ramparts of the
Rockies and offers the traveler pan-
oramic views of the Great Plains
stretching hundreds of miles to the
east. The line winds through horseshoe curves where high winds have
blown trains from the tracks. Hop-
per cars filled with ballast and
welded to the rails serve as a per-
manent windbreak.

A Missouri Pacific switch engine plies an industrial spur near the Great Salt Lake in Utah.

Leaving Walsenburg, Colorado, a
Burlington Northern freight passes
a pioneer cemetery against a backdrop of the Spanish Peaks of the
Sangre de Cristo Range.

A track worker (*left*) rides a primitive handcar through clear mountain air along the Cumbres and Toltec Scenic Railroad, one surviving portion of the Denver & Rio Grande Western's once extensive narrow-gauge operation in the Colorado Rockies. Running sixty-four miles and reaching an elevation of 10,015 feet, it is the highest steam railroad in the United States. In an updated version of a traditional image, an almost spotless engineer (*above*) oils the locomotive.

The importance of Ogden, Utah, as
a railroad center (here the Union
Pacific met the Southern Pacific)
is seen in the size of its station
and length of its platform. This
stop on the *Pioneer* is the closest
a passenger train today comes
to Promontory, where the first transcontinental railroad was
completed in 1869.

Travelers on the *Southwest Chief* glimpse scores of small western towns like Wagon Mound, New Mexico, named for the rock that pioneers compared with the shape of their covered wagons.

The Santa Fe boldly proclaims itself on the unadorned depot at Trinidad, Colorado, still a waiting and meeting place. From Trinidad, Santa Fe trains climb Raton Pass, also the path of the Santa Fe Trail and later of the interstate highway. At 3.5 percent, it is one of the steepest mainline grades in America.

The route of the *Sunset Limited* from New Orleans to Los Angeles passes through swamp and bayou country so wet that special pilings have to support the rail line. Famous for alligators and crayfish, this country was settled by Acadian French exiled from Nova Scotia 200 years ago.

The Huey P. Long Bridge, which crosses the Mississippi River above New Orleans, is the longest railroad bridge in the world: 23,235 feet. Seen here, the westbound *Sunset Limited* climbs the girdered approach. Before the bridge opened in 1935, all trains had to be ferried across the river.

THE WEST COAST

Collis P. Huntington, who along with Charles Crocker, Leland Stanford, and Mark Hopkins constituted California's Big Four. Together they made their Southern Pacific into a vast railroad empire that reached from Portland to New Orleans.

River valleys attract railroads. In America two of the most dramatic examples are the Hudson River Valley in the East and, here in the West, the Columbia River Gorge between Washington and Oregon. The most important stream in western North America, the Columbia cuts through the lava beds of the Cascade Mountains (here) under dizzying cliffs, 160 miles from the Pacific, where the sage-brush country gives way to coastal rain forest.

Unlike the Atlantic shore, which was the face that America presented to late-Renaissance Europeans searching for new worlds, the Pacific shore is not a welcoming one. The fact that its great natural harbors are just three — Seattle, San Francisco, and San Diego — was a key deterrent in a sea-going age. Settlement, when it did come, was more from the inside out than from the shore inland. In the long quiet years before the United States' presence overwhelmed all others in North America in the mid-nineteenth century, this far shore lay at the extremity of a European empire. The Russians, the British, and most importantly the Spanish, all touched it, and in the end all let it go. The main course of these powers' ambitions still lay elsewhere, on the Eurasian landmass and in the Atlantic Basin. The contours of the Pacific world had not yet truly been discerned, and they would not be until well into our own era. Once they were, it would become necessary to regard this place — shared by the states of Washington, Oregon, and California — both as the western edge of one world and the eastern edge of another. From the strictly American point of view, it was the last stop en route to many promised lands, its history marked more than most places by the search for fresh solutions and a faith in ever possible renewal.

Renewal is one word that might fairly describe the Southern Pacific passenger trains that once plied this coastal route. A glamour-run into the 1950s, then sadly run down in the 1960s, it is today one of Amtrak's great success stories. The Southern Pacific itself (whose rails Amtrak's *Coast Starlight* uses between Portland and Los Angeles) is one of America's and the West's great sagas of entrepreneurial and corporate derring-do. From an initial investment in 1860 of $1,500 each in the yet unbuilt Central Pacific Railroad, Mark Hopkins, Collis P. Huntington, Charles Crocker, and Leland Stanford parlayed a transportation and business empire unequaled in scale anywhere in America. Hopkins and Huntington were partners in a prosperous San Francisco hardware store; Crocker the owner of a dry-goods emporium; Stanford a wholesale grocer. Together they came to be revered or reviled as the Big Four, the archetypal robber barons, plutocrats, and monopolists of America's Gilded Age — but also empire builders, developers, and benefactors who built up a great region. To this day, memory of them is keen, and their names are ever-present on the landscape: the Mark Hopkins Hotel, the Crocker National Bank, the Huntington Library, Stanford University. The Southern Pacific, as their railroad soon came to be named, blanketed California, reached up to Oregon, east to Utah (the original Central Pacific line over the Sierras), and all the way across southern Arizona, New Mexico, and Texas to New Orleans. Its corporate logo depicted a railroad track receding, presumably, into a western sunset, and its timetables, among the fattest in the nation, offered dozens of trains along its four famous routes: the Sunset, the Overland, the Golden State, and the Shasta.

The Shasta Route, named for the famous Oregon peak, is the line you travel today between Portland and Oakland. The Southern Pacific actually has two parallel lines, a westerly one through Medford, Oregon, on what had once been the Oregon & California Railroad (the Siskiyou Line, known as the "Road of a Thousand Wonders"), and a newer, less rugged, but still highly scenic line to the east through Chemult and Klamath Falls, dubbed the Cascade Line. Forty and fifty years ago, before highway and air travel had intruded, there were five daily trains between California and the Northwest with regionally inspired names like *Rouge River, Klamath, Oregonian, Shasta Limited, Cascade.* The *Cascade* was the top train and, as it turned out, the longest survivor. Sumptuously equipped by Pullman in 1927, it lured high-toned travelers willing to pay the three-dollar extra fare for a twenty-three-hour, twenty-minute San Francisco–Portland run, which included the services of a barber, a valet, and a ladies' maid. The cars had shower baths and even intercar telephones. An equally luxurious streamlined version was introduced in 1950, on a schedule trimmed to just sixteen and a half hours, which is about what the trip takes today.

The 1950s version of the *Cascade* was still a luxury operation, catering to first-class clientele. Even as the tables of public taste and subsidy were turning decisively in favor of other forms of transport, the railroad companies spent millions of dollars to sustain the appeal of train travel. In the presence of trains like the *Cascade*, no one can say that the boys in the boardroom didn't give it one last grand try. To *Cascade* passengers in the 1950s they made available a handsome two-tone gray streamliner offering roomettes, bedrooms, compartments, and drawing rooms for the ultimate in all-private-room Pullman comfort. And as a train

Southern Pacific's *Shasta Limited* and *Cascade* carried the carriage trade between Portland and San Francisco in the days before airliners.

whose midafternoon departures from each terminal made for leisurely cocktails and dining, especially ample provision was made in the "Cascade Club," a 203-foot-long articulated diner and lounge. Full-width car connections gave the illusion of one enormous space that included a full-length club car with a stand-up semicircular bar amidships decorated in Northwest tones of blue, cedar, gold, and silver. The adjacent diner was configured with spacious tables, and was serviced by a large staff of waiters working from the galley in the third car. From the first dry martinis right through to the ritual finger bowls, it was very easy to spend several hours in such a splendid vehicle.

Before Amtrak, travel south down the coast to Los Angeles required a change of trains in Oakland. The Southern Pacific's headquarters was after all just across the Bay on Market Street in San Francisco, and the Bay Area had always been the heart of its operations, a disposition that dated from a time when southern California was still a sleepy Spanish backwater. But the south's legendary development, first in the 1920s and then after World War II, soon produced a high volume of traffic between its metropolis, Los Angeles, and this older one by the Golden Gate. It was a demand that, again, the Southern Pacific management met with panache, providing in the late 1930s what was widely agreed to be the world's most beautiful train along what many would have added was one of the world's most beautiful railroad lines. For 113 miles the Southern Pacific's coast line between the Bay Area and Los Angeles skirts the Pacific Ocean, the longest such run along any coast anywhere. The train was the *Daylight*, which endured in diminishing form right down to 1971. (The daylight schedule and thus the splendid view along the coast are still preserved in Amtrak's *Coast Starlight*.) In its heyday it sported a stunning livery: red, orange, and black on streamlined chair cars, parlor cars, diners, and lounges, on whose sides was emblazoned the special *Daylight* emblem: an orange California sun with wings suggesting speed. The great night train along the coast line through San Luis Obispo and Santa Barbara was the all-Pullman *Lark*, which over the years became the object of intense regional attachment (its emblem was a silver moon with wings), and whose discontinuance in the late 1960s was greeted with much protest and sadness. In the years when it was still in management's favor, the *Lark*, stylishly connecting the two greatest cities of this western coast, both of which are Californian to the core, offered a standard of service that was the Southern Pacific's and indeed California's riposte to the *Twentieth Century Limited* and other eastern contenders.

The Amtrak train that today traverses this long and lovely coastline is a curious thing. Its very name, *Coast Starlight*, is a hybrid culled from a sad chapter of Southern Pacific history: the original *Starlight* was an all-coach night counterpart to the *Daylight* on the coast line, which soon succumbed to California's growing lust for freeways. Amtrak touts it, quite rightly, as one of its finest runs, with through service from Seattle to Los Angeles past some very grand scenery. Clearly it is one of Amtrak's busiest trains; sleeping-car space is hard to come by, and the coaches run near to capacity year-round. It connects four major metropolises, and a lot of college towns in between, and its passengers reflect the especially wide range of social types that today is a hallmark of America's West Coast. Though the atmosphere on any Amtrak train is decidedly casual (except perhaps on the Metroliners in the Northeast Corridor), on

The open observation platform, once a feature of every first-class train in America, here graces the Southern Pacific's *Shasta Limited*. Open platforms vanished with the fashion of streamlining in the 1940s and 1950s; the only ones in service today are privately owned.

the *Coast Starlight* it is more casual than most — and therefore least like a passenger train as traditionally remembered. Things don't fit: admonition over the PA system against the use of pipes and cigars, and against going barefoot between the cars; two young men en route to San Francisco, obviously on a budget, who brought their food with them (a whole turkey in an ice chest, which they proceeded to enjoy in the middle of the lounge car to loud conversation about football); a pensioner who brought his own bottled manhattans rather than buy from the management; young people in their twenties who, it would seem, stepped right out of the 1960s. The management condones all, as in a sense it must; Amtrak is a very democratic agency. Besides, this is the market, and the market has come a long way from the well-heeled businessmen and their ladies who once took their manhattans poured from a shaker in the "Cascade Club."

People who value the quantity of their time (or whose employers value it) — that is, the business expense-account crowd — simply do not travel by train anymore and likely never will again. So if you wear a jacket and tie to the diner, the only other person similarly dressed will likely be the steward (or "lead service attendant" in the most current locution) — and the steward may well be a woman. If you tip the porter (again, the "attendant" as he or she is now called), you will again have distinguished yourself from most passengers who are unacquainted with this time-honored concluding ritual of any Pullman journey. Today the carriage trade is 30,000 feet up, enjoying "business class" while eating dinner on its lap. With the patronage thus gone elsewhere, Amtrak's notion of first class is, plausibly, somewhat diminished. Still, the staff, overtaxed as it is, tries hard and deserves much praise. With more to work with, and another class of passenger to serve, some of them would truly shine.

The trip today southward out of Seattle offers a bedlam of West Coast images: the great Boeing aircraft works with a Second World War B-17 parked next to an AWACS reconaissance jet; the sadly abandoned Tacoma station with its still glorious copper dome; a waterfront with ships from Hong Kong and eateries hawking Chilean sea bass and shark. You have a handsome view of the Tacoma Narrows Suspension Bridge (whose predecessor collapsed dramatically in a windstorm in 1940), and skirting Puget Sound an eyeful of the colors of the Northwest: evergreens, gray lowering skies, and the blue water of this great inland arm of

the Pacific. Across the Columbia River where the Southern
Pacific begins, Portland, Oregon, presents a station largely
untouched by the ravages of the last thirty years. Trains
from Seattle, Spokane, Salt Lake City, and San Francisco
still call here, and their passengers are greeted by a finely
maintained brick edifice topped with a tower in which the
Roman-numeraled clock still keeps time and from which
the flag still flies. Detraining passengers quickly discover
what region they are now in as they pass a nine-and-a-half-
foot-diameter slice of nine-hundred-year-old fir tree dis-
played on the platform. In the waiting room, riches of a
man-made sort attend them: the Pringle Family Union News
Stand and functioning red-orange neon signs that guide
you, in the idiom of another era, to "Parcels, Cigars, Lounge,
Baggage Room, and Stationmaster." Compared to degraded
King Street Station in Seattle, Portland's is a proud example of a proper, still-working, medium-sized railroad station, of which there are few remaining in America.

Leaving the station, the train veers sharply to the right,
across a massive double-deck vertical lift bridge over the

In the 1940s Southern Pacific's
streamlined *Daylight*, which ran
between Los Angeles and San Francisco, was with good reason touted
as the most beautiful train in the
world.

Willamette River, and passes grain boats from far ports. The fertile and temperate Willamette Valley was what first drew American settlers here in the 1830s and 1840s, across the plains and over the Oregon Trail. In Salem, first the territorial and then the state capital, the "Golden Pioneer" stands atop the capitol building memorializing this particular great American trek. West lies the Coast Range, which separates the valley from the beautiful but barren Pacific shore. From Eugene to Dunsmuir, California, lie 300 miles of heavy-duty mountain railroad, as the line ascends some 3,600 feet to Cascade Summit, top of the range and a notoriously snowy place in winter. Mount Shasta, an extinct volcano and namesake of the route, looms up 14,160 feet out in the darkness. Farther off lies another volcano, now filled with water and called Crater Lake.

Sacramento, California's capital, comes at 6:00 A.M.; Davis, with its mission-style depot, palms, and evergreens, at 6:20; Oakland and salt water at breakfast. Though the train now runs through down the coast to southern California, this is where the west-coast journey ends for many, just as it literally divided for the Southern Pacific passengers who years ago changed here from the *Cascade* to the *Lark*.

South from the Bay Area, the Southern Pacific's coast line does not actually reach the coast for 250 miles, but first passes through the rich fruit and vegetable country of the Salinas Valley: black soil, endless green fields of lettuce, gangs of stoop labor in yellow rain gear. Around Castroville, the artichoke capital of the world, the plants bearing that strange and wonderful fruit arouse bemused guesses as to their identity from the city folk on board who recognize an artichoke only if it is served up under plastic wrap at the supermarket, while on sidings sit the Pacific Fruit Express refrigerator cars that will take the artichokes to just such markets. Stenciled on their sides, the identification "Crocker Citizens National Bank Trustee" recalls a California heritage much older here than the artichoke is. A hundred miles farther on, the Franciscan Mission of San Miguel, adjacent to the railroad and with its picture-perfect adobe, red tile, and cactus, recalls an older one yet, indeed the oldest European heritage on this coast and a reminder that this was once the path of El Camino Real, the Royal or the King's Highway. The king was the king of Spain, and the highway really only a horse path connecting the string of mission outposts that in the eighteenth century secured for crown and cross what to the Spanish was Alta or Upper California. While the influence of the cross endured, Spain held this far province of empire only loosely, and when the moment came, as it did in the mid-nineteenth century, their Mexican heirs proved no match for the hordes of treasure-hunting Yankees whose lightning appearance and determined avaricious ways helped bring California into the Union in 1850.

Between here and San Luis Obispo the railroad crests the Coast Range, over which it must pass to reach the sea. It is one of America's most dramatic railroad rides, through Tunnel Number Six and down the Cuesta grade. The cloud-shrouded peaks might be the Andes; below, rounded brown hills with odd clumps of trees constitute a landscape unique to this mountain-coastal region. Descending to San Luis Obispo (which is the station for William Randolph Hearst's San Simeon, one of the man-made wonders of this place), the train negotiates a horseshoe curve nearly as showy as the older, more famous one back east in Pennsylvania. South of San Luis Obispo the line finally reaches its name-sake shore, which it follows for the 113 miles to Santa Barbara. Some of this can only be seen by train, and it offers a view of the western edge of this continent as if untouched from the time when the Spanish fathers and the Indians before them first beheld it. While cattle now graze domestically down to the beach and far off-shore an occasional oil rig and tanker service the new age, it is difficult not to be moved by what appears the timeless spilling of a large empty land down into an even larger and emptier sea. The cliffs in places could be Cornwall, but the beaches they slowly give way to could only be the American West Coast. South of Santa Barbara, with its 1905 mission-style station and enormous Australian fig tree, people crowd in, their RVs parked bumper to bumper all along the sea wall. Highways soon are everywhere, the sure sign that Los Angeles, home of the freeway, cannot be far.

Los Angeles is now, in fact, America's second city, having a few years ago nudged Chicago from that dubiously enviable position. The two places are not, however, really comparable except in terms of crude arithmetic. Chicago is a heavy-duty place, an industrial and commercial power-house where things are made and traded, a crossroads metropolis between East and West where even in the age of the "service economy" the old Sandburg images still exert enormous power. Los Angeles is tinsel town, as they say, whose suprisingly rich social reality never quite manages to transcend the old technicolor Hollywood image. Today in

Passengers bound for San Francisco from the north or the east went only as far as Oakland by rail, whence steam ferries like the *Eureka* (California's state motto) completed the journey to the Golden Gate.

its heyday, it is an automobile town. Chicago in its (which was some time ago) was a railroad town, and it had the great stations to prove it. It does no longer. There is in this something, beyond just numbers, that confirms Los Angeles's new-found status as number two. For Los Angeles still possesses, and uses as such, what is today the second finest intact railroad terminal in America, after Grand Central in New York City. Chicago had half a dozen as recently as the 1960s; today only half of Union Station remains and even it is threatened by controversial redevelopment. Los Angeles only ever had one of grand stature, and it still has it.

Los Angeles Union Passenger Terminal (LAUPT as it was known to an earlier age, much as LAX is common airline parlance today) is where you will arrive on the *Coast Starlight* from Seattle, Portland, and Oakland. And from it you can depart on other trains across mountains and deserts and along coastlines to Salt Lake City and Denver, to Albuquerque and Kansas City; to Tucson and San Antonio, to San Juan Capistrano and San Diego. The product of much wrangling between city boosters intent on achieving a fitting gateway to their booming city, and the cantankerous railroads that served it, LAUPT opened to great civic festivity in May 1939. It was still a prosperous time for the passenger train, and the half-million people who turned out for the opening parade, which was set to the theme of "Railroads Build the Nation," were given every reason to think it would long remain so. An historical pageant depicted the role of the railroads in the building of the West, while the three lines that shared the new station proudly paraded their latest hardware. Huge locomotives of the Santa Fe, Union Pacific, and Southern Pacific lumbered past the reviewing stand bedecked with flags and banners proclaiming "Future Prosperity" and "Continued Cooperation." Hollywood naturally got into the act and actually preempted the first departure from LAUPT with a special train sent around the country to promote Paramount's just-released cinematic epic, *Union Pacific*. Posing before a rehabilitated Virginia & Truckee diamond-stack steamer built in 1873, Los Angeles mayor Fletcher Brown and Union Pacific president W.M. Jeffers were joined by George Raft, Lloyd Nolan, and Cecil B. deMille himself in the perfect evocation of the movies' and the railroads' golden years.

"Dedicated to the spirit of private enterprise and the continuing growth of southern California," as the opening day rhetoric put it (the railroads, not the city, footed the construction bill), LAUPT did make a fine gateway to what was

The Southern Pacific's Portland-to-Oakland *Cascade* in 1944.

and would remain for years a booming city and region. That the railroads would not long share in that bright future could not then be foreseen, but it hardly matters. For they gave to Los Angeles and to train travelers to this day a splendid monument in stucco and tile to the way southern California at its best chose to see itself. It was above all meant to be an efficiently functioning modern railroad terminal, which it was, handling at its peak in the 1940s sixty-six arrivals and departures daily. But its form — early California mission complete with landscaped courtyards and set 200 feet back from the street on what was known as the Plaza Site adjacent to where the city was founded — conjured up the old pre-Hollywood fantasy of Franciscan fathers and old Californios before the Yankees came. From the street, you enter through a fifty-foot-high arch rimmed with colored mosaics and patterned glass and pass into an immense entrance vestibule. To the left opens the ticket concourse, the station's largest space, with a lofty wood-beamed ceiling and 115-foot-long ticket counter fashioned from American black walnut. Natural light pours through arched windows with iron grill-work. Straight ahead, the main waiting room beckons with leather-upholstered settees, red quarry-tile floors edged in marble strips suggesting a carpet runner, amber cathedral glass windows, and Spanish-style chandeliers ten feet in diameter.

There was a time, into the 1950s, when all this was

Southern Pacific's *Oakland Lark* in streamlined livery in the late 1940s. This train succumbed early to California's lust for freeways.

familiar territory to reporters, press agents, and assorted advance men who waited for Gable or Garland, Crosby or Monroe to alight from Santa Fe's legendary *Super Chief* or Union Pacific's *City of Los Angeles* after the three-day voyage from New York via Chicago's Pump Room and Ambassador East. The railroads' readiness to cash in on the glamour of the southern California–Hollywood connection is caught forever in their promotional literature of that day, an especially fine example of which featured then movie actor Ronald Reagan dining under glass in one of the *City of Los Angeles* dome-diners of the 1950s, testifying that "traveling by Domeliner is one of the happiest habits I've ever acquired." Humbler folk, presumably many fans and aspiring starlets among them, arrived on humbler trains like the *Scout* and the *Californian*; during World War II, countless soldiers, sailors, and airmen alighted here from troop sleepers en route to the region's defense installations and then to battlegrounds of the South Pacific. Together they filled these great halls to capacity, ate everything the Fred Harvey restaurant had to offer, and dropped endless nickels and dimes in the wooden booths of the telephone room, which in the days before direct dialing was serviced by the station's own switchboard. Today the celebrities and the great luxury trains and Fred Harvey are gone, but substantial crowds of ordinary travelers can still be found here, on the same settees, waiting for an Amtrak departure.

"Traveling by domeliner is one of the happiest habits I've ever acquired!"

Ronald Reagan

UNION PACIFIC RAILROAD

Domeliner "CITY OF LOS ANGELES"

AMERICA'S FINEST TRAIN • DAILY TO CHICAGO

The Union Pacific's "domeliners" of the 1950s and 1960s featured a dining room under glass and a breakfast of kippers ($1.60), brook trout ($3.25), or lamb chops ($3.50). It was enough to make a future president smile.

Their numbers are of course diminished, but still adequate to give this, the last-built of the great stations, a respectable future in the job it was designed for.

Of all the major places you can get to from LAUPT, San Diego can be reached on any of the seven daily trains, better service in fact than the Santa Fe offered back in the 1940s. One hundred twenty-eight miles to the south, this is the end of the journey down the west coast, and it is a good place to finish. Its own fine mission-style station, still proudly emblazoned "Santa Fe," looks out onto the Embarcadero and San Diego Bay. There you can find moored, also from another age, the bark *Star of India*, still seaworthy, rigged, and ready to make sail — the oldest merchantman afloat. From our own age, you are likely to find, if the fleet is in, a cruiser or aircraft carrier home from Pacific patrol. The line that brought you here belongs to the Santa Fe, and it hugs the coast from San Juan Capistrano through Oceanside and San Clemente. Known as the Surf Line, it is a lovely

As far south on the West Coast as the train will take you, San Diego beckons with its monumental mission-style station and, across the bay, the palatial Del Coronado Hotel. The train's name was, and is, appropriately, the *San Diegan*.

ride. The Santa Fe reached the Pacific at San Diego just over a century ago, in 1883. Two years later railroad tycoon Elisha Babcock bought 4,100 acres across the bay in Coronado and began to realize his dream of a resort hotel that would be "the talk of the western world." The Del Coronado still stands, one of the largest wooden structures in the world and one of its finest remaining examples of Victorian resort architecture. Few guests now arrive by train over at San Diego's old Spanish station. ("Fifteen minutes from the San Diego International Airport" is what the hotel brochure notes.) For a place of such vintage and distinction this is sad but hardly surprising. That "The Del" has so long outlived the railroad age that produced it is itself remarkable enough here in California, the land of endless renewal. But its guestrooms and spacious public halls are routinely filled to capacity; its beaches still tempt visitors from Nashville, Minneapolis, and Texarkana to test the Pacific waters. Overhead the Stars and Stripes flies from its cupola, as if this really were an outpost, and as far as continental America was meant to go.

Between Santa Barbara and San
Luis Obispo, the *Coast Starlight*
hovers above the Pacific shore for
113 miles, the longest coastline run
of a passenger train anywhere in
the world.

California's thousand-mile-long
coastline, part of which is seen here
at Point Conception, is bold, rugged,
and famous for surf.

Left: One of a series of extinct volcanoes on the West Coast, Oregon's Mount Shasta was a favorite backdrop for publicity photos of famous Southern Pacific trains such as the *Shasta Daylight*. Today's train traveler, however, must be content to view it by moonlight.

Above: For many miles in western America, the isolated rails pass through virtual wilderness.

The West Coast is known for its
benign climate and unconventional
styles of living. In Seattle, Washington, an old caboose (*above*) becomes
a home; in San Juan di Capistrano,
California, the view from the station platform (*right*) opens onto
another western fantasy.

Above: The old Hollywood fantasy of Spanish California meets the railroad age in the tile and stucco interior of Los Angeles Union Passenger Terminal, whose sunlit halls welcomed the world to southern California.

Right: Los Angeles Union Passenger Terminal evoked the mission style at its most grandiose. Opened in 1939 to much civic fanfare, it was a true "union" station, for it brought all rail lines serving the city into one terminal. It beckoned movie moguls and common folk alike with lofty wood-beamed ceilings, leather settees, Spanish-style chandeliers, and landscaped courtyards. Today the moguls are all gone, but the station still serves.

Preceding pages: Commuter trains from San Francisco travel as far south as San Jose and are powered by 3,000-horsepower F40 diesel locomotives, the workhorses of American passenger trains. Chevrons enhance visibility at grade crossings.

Above: Engineer (left) and conductor of a *San Diegan* take their ease in the landscaped courtyard of Los Angeles Union Passenger Terminal before departure time.

From the railroad's clifftop vantage,
bright sand, surf, and tanning bod-
ies give the feeling of low flying.
Beach life is more associated with
California than anywhere in the
world except perhaps Australia.

Perhaps the finest of the small mission-style stations in southern California, Glendale *(above and right)* is immaculately maintained by the station agent. Partly true to history and partly conjured by Hollywood, the Spanish motif was typical of how California once chose to see itself.

Following pages: Piles of white nitrate will help make the Salinas Valley green with lettuces and artichokes, shipped by rail to the rest of America.

Fresh flowers—though they no longer grace the dining-car table—are a cash crop in Washington. The *Coast Starlight* skirts fields of spring daffodils and glacier-faced Mount Rainier.

The neon sign proclaiming a non-existent "Fountain" at Amtrak's Oakland, California, station recalls an old railroad tradition. The station restaurant was once a fixture of all large American railroad stations and many smaller ones. In the nineteenth century, before the advent of the dining car, meal stops were common. Today in Oakland it's pocket books, postcards, and coffee: the "sundries" of the eighties.

Go.

Union Station, Portland, Oregon.

ACKNOWLEDGEMENTS

Gracious thanks are due to John McLeod, Sue Martin, Debbie Marciniak, and Arthur Lloyd of Amtrak for their arrangement of travel across the Amtrak system. To Chuck Forsman of Boulder, Colorado, and the Ronald Jacobson family of Crosby, North Dakota, go thanks for the guidance only natives can give. Several books have been especially valuable and are recommended for further reading: Lucius Beebe and Charles Clegg, *The Trains We Rode*, 2 vols. (San Francisco: Howell-North Books 1965–66); Arthur D. Dubin, Some Classic Trains (Milwaukee: Kalbach Publishing, 1964) and *More Classic Trains* (1974); Ira Fistell, *America by Train* (New York, Burt Franklin & Co., Inc.). Past schedules come from *The Official Guide of the Railways*, published monthly by the National Railway Publication Co. in New York.